IT'S G

Words of wisdom can be found in the most unlikely places!

From a book on *Atheism* we read that Spirituality is not just good for your soul but good for your mind as well.

It can make you Happy, Peaceful and even Wise, and from an unlikely source, a heartbroken electrician, when his dog passed away, expressed his great sadness to him (the dog) with the words:

"So long, Barney, see you in the next world."

It's God's Magic

by

Mary Bowmaker

All best wishes to all at the Alister Hardy library.

Mary Bowmaker.
(Jan. 2022)

COURTENBEDE

ABOUT THE AUTHOR

A FORMER PROFESSIONAL MUSICIAN, both teacher and performer, Mary Bowmaker has always loved writing, small successes over the years encouraging and inspiring her to write her first book *A Little School on the Downs*; a record of the life and work of a headmistress and her school in Victorian England. *Is Anybody There, Leaning on the Invisible,* and *The Reality of the Unbelievable* are her first three books about the paranormal.

This book is dedicated, as always, to my wonderful, darling parents

Mary and Stephen Wilton

and to

My Beloved Husband Peter R. Bowmaker

and Toby, our unbeatable Yorkshire terrier

CONTENTS

ACKNOWLEDGEMENTS

My thanks to:

Special thanks to, as always, 'The Religious Experience Research Centre, carrying on with their research into religious experiences, archiving their accounts of the experience and making them available to researchers everywhere.

And thanks to the many people who are not afraid to speak out about their own experiences, giving hope and confidence to others who would otherwise have perhaps been 'shy' of asking or telling.

To friends everywhere for their interest, encouragement and support in my endeavours, always appreciated, and to Jane Tatam publisher, always ready to help, a big thank you.

Sincerely,

Mary Bowmaker

FOREWORD

The Nation Prayed. Not once did the nation pray, but 'seven' times over the next six years.

Eight months into the Second World War and now, May 26th 1940, the situation was desperate, so desperate that the country 'was called' to prayer, by no less an authority than the King, King George VI, and Parliament.

Time spills over and 'over and over' passing as 'nothing'. Now, today, not that I want to remind us all of what we have been through over the past challenging months, but from the start of this pandemic (no need for dates), we now know the worry, the stresses, the horror of it all for many. This included hundreds of children we know are suffering with mental health problems.

Surely I am not the only one to want to ask the Powers that Be when will we hear the call for prayer? A prayer for 'strength and guidance' during this ordeal. There are 'countless' 'denominations', but only one True God who cares about each and every one of us. Where was the call to prayer as in the Second World War, why has it not come…because it never was.

(Written from the heart by Mary Bowmaker)

God's Magic

'All embracing; running through every
beat of life, every circumstance, both in
nature and in human kind; in the seen
and unseen worlds, often unnoticed.'

CHAPTER ONE

Making Contact

This Sceptered Isle,
This precious stone set in a silver sea,
This Blessed Plot,
This Earth,
THIS ENGLAND.

May 26th 1940

THE NATION PRAYED. NOT once did the nation pray, but
seven times over the next six years. Eight months into the Second
World War and now, May 26th, 1940, the situation was desperate;
so desperate, that the country was called to prayer by no less an
authority than the King, King George VI, and Parliament.

The nation prayed, and the nation was answered, with seven
miraculous events that heralded the turning point in a war the

enemy believed we were fated to lose; the result of that would have been for the whole world to have been damned, plunged into a terrible darkness. So dire were our circumstances, with food stocks, fuel, weaponry, aircraft, supplies of *all* necessities running low (or out), that we *had* to turn to a superior source, the final source to be called on by humanity since the beginning of time; 'God'.

The nation prayed; the people as one throughout the land. From the grandeur of Westminster Abbey to the humblest church or abode, or no abode, there was such a cramming in and a spilling over of perplexed, worried, frightened citizens commandeering every space, every street, station, town centre, countryside, all determined to be part of this mass prayer phenomenon they were called on to hold. And pray they did! All denominations, believers, and nonbelievers alike, prayed together, as one.

May 26th, 1940, the first call on the nation to prayer, then the first miracle, the miracle of Dunkirk. Dunkirk. How can we speak that name in even tones knowing the history, the story, a story of heartbreak and sheer despair? Tragedy; TRAGEDY, turned to 'perhaps'; perhaps to 'uplift'; uplift to 'can we', followed by determination, then 'hope'.

Through holding on to hope, and courage, and with the confidence of prayer, a proud, selfless nation united, rallied, giving us a story never bettered in the annals of history; a story so fraught with the horrific echoes of what 'might have been', now galvanised into what became a 'glorious glory of the first degree'.

This story, the miracle of Dunkirk, has been well reported and recorded in every form of communication possible; you will probably know it, and, along with every other person familiar with it, react in complete amazement and absorption 'again and again' even at just the thought of it all. 'Feel the feelings' as I do, want to sit and reflect on it all. So now, partly because you will know it, and to avoid (from me), an 'emotional take-over', can I simply out-line the events of the time, while together, you and I, recognise, and symbolically, bow our heads, to the might of the human spirit, and to the reality of 'The power of prayer'.

DUNKIRK, the story

Unprepared for war, we, the people of Britain, were in a 'totally desperate situation'; a 'catastrophic' situation', made worse by the fact that France had fallen to the Germans, and our British Army of 350,000 men were hemmed in with backs to the sea, at Dunkirk.

The German High Command was boasting that 'the British Army is encircled and our troops are proceeding to its annihilation'.

Meanwhile, back home, Britain had only our 'cobbled together' local defence force of volunteers. The Home Guard, volunteers who defended the five thousand miles of Britain's coastline; the ARP (Air Raid Precautions), and other groups of volunteers who banded together to help in any way possible. Volunteers, practising drill with broomsticks! Today, many of us, young and old alike, thoroughly enjoy the antics and banter of *Dad's Army* on television; the series returns year after year, remaining one of the most popular shows on TV and in the theatre. Behind all the high jinks and bumbling around that we love is the greatest respect and admiration for those 'real characters' of yesteryear, who were 'there', ready and willing to sacrifice life and limb... but to return to the story.

Before calling the nation to the first National Day of Prayer, Winston Churchill, the Prime Minister, spoke to the country in the most sombre of tones, explaining that he 'had hard and heavy tidings to announce'; The Commander of the British Forces, General Sir Frederick Morgan, said there was no way out (for our army from Dunkirk), barring a miracle.

Sunday, May 26th, His Majesty King George VI, and Parliament, called the people of Britain and The Empire to the first National Day of Prayer.

The Nation responded. The Nation was at prayer…Three Miracles then happened.

1. Hitler stopped his general advance.
2. A mighty, ferocious storm of extraordinary fury grounded the German air Force.
3. A great calm settled over the English Channel for several days—

338,000 men in the British Army were 'rescued', evacuated from Dunkirk.

A GREAT CALM SETTLED over the English Channel for several days, allowing 338,000 men of the British Army to be 'saved', rescued, evacuated from Dunkirk. How could this be? How could such a tremendous, unparalleled undertaking possibly happen? We had neither spare ships, nor man- power nor fuel… it was impossible…it would have to be a 'miracle of miracles'! And so it was.

Again, the nation was 'called on', but not this time for prayer, but for ships; big ships, little ships, small boats, any boats, 'manned', with fuel, all ready to go, Destination, Dunkirk; and what a response. Here is where my sense of feeling really kicks in). Can you see it, can you picture it, could you burst with pride, surely, 'yes'?

Most of the following details are from Commander E. Keble Chatterton.

Things happened quickly. Immense possibilities widened, resulting from a *'marvel of detailed organisation'*. Already the Admiralty had, with great foresight, given notice that all privately owned motor craft of 30 to 100 feet in length were to be at their disposal.

At least one amateur yachtsman and his son sailed their yacht from Southampton to Dunkirk on their own initiative, and brought home a batch of tired, weary soldiers.

The Ministry of Shipping was aware of movements of craft, and so could lay its hands on suitable vessels almost instantly. Telephoning and telegraphing soon brought together a vast, improvised fleet of nearly 1,000! Nothing like it 'had ever been seen before'. Can you imagine it...

From Trawlers, Drifters, Thames sailing and motor-barges, to small cargo carriers, colliers, motor boats and motor yachts. Royal National Life boats; open skiffs; oared boats from liners, sailing boats from South end beach, tugs from the Thames. Six motor 'bawleys', used to gather up cockles from the estuary. There were pleasure paddle steamers from the Clyde, from Llandudno, Margate.

Life boats, fire boats, steam yachts that were 'veterans', when fighting U-boats in the First World War were all there; Dutch schooners, ships from Belgian naval units. Cross-channel steamers with plenty of passenger accommodation and high speed, AND volunteers to 'man' the boats which would be used as ferries, lifting our soldiers from the beach to the safety of the waiting ships. The list goes on and on until it numbered 665 craft, in addition to 222 naval units.

Big ships, little ships, small boats, any boats...while the sea, the English Channel, remained as calm as a milk pond when thousands, 338,000 men, of the British Expeditionary Army, were rescued from the sands of Dunkirk.

All ships forever and affectionately known as 'The Little Ships of Dunkirk'.

A readers' comment on the story of the Second World War: 'I don't think many people, and even many Christians, realise the spiritual implications surrounding WWII, and I read that Churchill's bodyguard, and though not a Christian himself, noted Churchill's reliance and trust in God throughout the entire war.'

Robert, a nice young man who works in our local computer shop, was amazed when I told him about my research into the Second World War, and the fact that the whole nation was 'called to prayer' by the King and Parliament, seven times. I mentioned reading that the people had responded brilliantly to the call, crowds – here Robert interrupted me with a strong 'huh, I bet they wouldn't do that now', his words prompting me to an equally strong reply, 'I think they would.'

Thinking about Robert's words, and my answer, brought me back to my query over findings I had discovered in a little research I completed recently. Although looking to record the experiences of people in the (so-called) paranormal, instead of experiences, one after the other were giving me a real feeling of 'awareness'; a belief, a questioning, was it perhaps a 'sense' that was there with them though not yet quite understood; a strong feeling that there was a 'something' or somebody, with them. A personal, 'all knowing' intelligence that could advise, assure, comfort, dissuade, reprimand… (Could this last one be 'conscience'?) Then there was a sometimes strong feeling that we <u>are</u> *more* than this physical body we inhabit while here on the earth plane

There is a rising tide of consciousness leading to a flood of understanding, an awakening, as Sir George Trevelyan, one of the great pioneers of 'New Age Thinking', in this our new age of Aquarius, tells us.

An 'awakening', and that is what I feel I was sensing, I was seeing, I was reading, in one experience after another; an awakening to an awareness which we have almost lost (but never will), having lain dormant over time, our attention focused almost wholly on the physical, the material.

Perhaps a good example of people reporting on having strong

'feelings', strong thoughts about say, 'life in general'; 'dreams' that are often a good guide as to what to do in a certain situation (as we read about in the Bible), and so on, resonated with me when listening to John. He tried to explain (and Margaret, his wife, was listening), the thoughts and feelings she often expressed and how, over the years, he had learnt to rely – for decisions on all sorts of things – but he could never understand these feelings of hers, that is, until recently.

John and Margaret took a day trip to Northumberland to visit Flodden Field, the historic site of the famous Battle of Flodden, in 1513. It was the scene of a fierce battle, the longest one fought between the two kingdoms of England and Scotland during which King James IV of Scotland was 'killed', the Scottish Army, defeated. John positioned himself in the middle, as far as he could judge, of the field, and immediately as he stood there, was 'almost overcome' with the strangest, strongest, emotions he had ever known. He had not thought himself capable of such 'emotions', 'feelings', but he knew they were real. As to why this happened, he is still in the dark, but certainly a lot wiser and understanding of the whys and wherefores when his wife insists on a certain thing, because, as she so regularly points out, she just 'knows'.

Joe, now nearing retirement age, has never forgotten, in his teens, a school trip to the Lake District. A group of them, all teenagers, were camping, and on this particular day, they were enjoying a trip out with one of the teachers. Driving up hill and down dale, around tight corners with winding roads that seemed never ending, it was all very exciting and as if they were the only people in the world – or in the Lake District anyway. Joe was sitting next to the teacher who was driving, and he will never know why he said it, but he suddenly cautioned the teacher, 'Mr Anderson, there will be someone on the road around the next bend,' and sure enough there was. This 'prediction' was a once only in Joe's life but real enough, and strong enough, for him to *never* forget.

When he was five or six, Robert remembers talking to a man and woman who visited him at home, and when his parents, who overheard him talking to someone, questioned him about it, he gave them their name and description. It happened to be that they were his grandparents; they had been 'passed away' for years, but Robert knew nothing about them. On another occasion, his parents rushed into his bedroom on hearing an unusual noise. Finding him ill, they acted quickly, got immediate help, and so saved his life.

If you think about it carefully, you must have had experiences, times in your own life, even if only one, when you were led, guided into a certain decision or situation that changed everything and on looking back at it, you thought, in amazement, 'How did all that come about, how did it happen!'

An interesting programme on the radio recently featured successful scientist Sheila Rowan, who is working to prove – in fact she is leading the hunt to prove, the existence of gravitational waves. Her talk led on to 'instincts', intuition, and was of particular interest to me especially when she emphasised to people, young scientists, anyone, to 'Trust your instinct, your intuition.' Of course this is an important part of our make-up, of our 'feelings', of you and of me; all part of our essence, of the way we present ourselves, can connect with each other, and with the world beyond.

(Always listen to the message, your inner message, from the real you, remembering we are spirit here and now in a physical body, and not a physical body with a spirit).

(*'Beyond your physical self, beyond your thoughts and emotions, there lies a realm within you that is pure potential; from this place anything and everything is possible. Even miracles. Especially miracles.)*

'A miracle was reported in the North East Oct 2016; three-year-old Dylan, with a rare form of lung cancer, made a miraculous recovery. He recovered just before his life support machine was about to be turned off.'

Sylvia's experience here recorded not perhaps a miracle, but remarkable enough and important enough to have left its mark on a life forever. Sylvia, telling of the way a special picture 'fell'; the picture meant a lot to her, not broken, but just in the way that it fell – there was 'something', about it, and she continues, 'I have felt a hand brush over my hair – *strongly.*'

Eileen: 'If I send out a strong thought when rushed and worried and really needed, for a parking space, I always find one. This happened three times in one day.'

A man waiting for a bus in London suddenly changed his mind, deciding to walk. It saved his life.

Malcolm, living away from home, was in a state about his father who was seriously ill, and could 'pass away' at anytime. He sent thoughts out to his dad, asking him to somehow let him know when he had (passed/died). Within a day or two of these 'thoughts', one night, the phone never stopped ringing. There was no one there. On and on it rang, all night, no one answering; then he realised, he just knew, it was his dad letting him know that he had 'gone'. Malcolm found out later that he had, and so sent out the thought, the reply 'message received'.

An awakening; people now looking at certain incidents, happenings, even simple, seemingly 'trivialities' – 'I found a leaf on the garden path in the shape of a perfect heart, and I knew immediately it was a sign that my mother was with me', *seemingly trivialities, but can mean everything.*

The rising tide of consciousness, giving us a new understanding – even with a Tarot Card.

Allan, a taxi driver, after his divorce, met another woman, Anne, and although each enjoyed each other's company, had no intention, either of them, of moving on to anything more serious. Time passed, and one evening, perhaps for a bit of fun, Anne had a Tarot Card reading. It was explained to her that the cards would be shuffled, moved around, and finally, the one that was 'turned, facing up' would mean something to her. The card turned up was 'the fool'.

Allan didn't believe in such things at the time, but he was quite shaken when she told him about her message through the cards – and that 'the fool', April 1st would mean something to her; it certainly meant something to Allan, it was his birthday. Allan and Anne did stay together, and have remained so, happily, for years.

'Thoughts', 'feelings', and 'seeing'; June tells us of her brother Michael who swears he does not believe in anything other than the material; what he can see and touch, yet he also swears by the one real experience that happened in his life many years ago.

His brother Norman was a sailor in the merchant navy, during the Second World War, on a ship that sank; it was torpedoed, and most of the crew including Norman, were lost.

On the night of the tragedy, Norman appeared, standing at his bedside. Forever after, Norman's mantra was, 'I don't believe in anything but—! (How many times have we heard those words?)

Watching a kitchen light bulb, hanging on a long flex, swing backwards and forwards, around, up and down, repeating itself, swinging on and on for no apparent reason, held Jacquie transfixed; there was nothing anywhere near for this to happen, but it did.

Feeling especially low at this time, not long after her teenage son had been murdered and she was about to leave her home in Alabama, America, on a teacher exchange plan with England, Jacquie wondered. In all the years she had lived in the house, nothing like this had ever happened; she pondered, and at the same time felt a tiny smile warm her mouth and her heart give a few tiny leaps of, was it 'joy'? Could this be a way of, perhaps a form of, 'communication', from…her son? It would fit in with his sense of mischief, his sense of fun. Half accepting this thought, whatever it was certainly helped her over the following difficult weeks, as she made her way to, and tried to settle, in England.

Jacquie soon found that the English teacher, under whose

wing she was 'entrusted', was a student of the 'paranormal'. The two of them quickly bonded, a firm friendship was forged, and happier times were ahead for Jacquie. Jacquie always believed, anyway, that it was the swinging light bulb, as it brought an 'ease' of heartache, a possibility of 'hope' that there must be 'something' out there, a something that cares enough to draw our attention to the 'strange', the impossible, and then to the strong belief, of her son's survival – that meant 'everything' to her.

We, you and I, are beginning to think seriously about, and accept and *feel* the influence of a far greater power than we ourselves (and the scientists) could ever project here on the earth plane; *'A rising tide of consciousness leading to a flood of understanding, an awakening'!* It is almost as if – is it similar to the reaction of our nation in the Second World War responding so brilliantly to the nations call to prayer? Is it through the circumstances we find ourselves in – circumstances found in the whole of the world; the turmoil, the grief, the cruelty, unfairness, 'upside-down-ness', of Everything.

As someone in the news media recently reported, referring to the war in Syria, 'There has been a complete melt down of humanity.'

'The Age of Aquarius!' Yes, we are definitely feeling the pull of Aquarius, and we have to persevere in these circumstances, with all the bumps along the way that change brings; until we absorb, suddenly become awake to an almighty surge of awareness, of Phenomena such as we have never before seen; it will happen. It has to happen. We have to change our ways, all of us, to putting the spiritual 'first and foremost' in life… and what does it mean to be 'spiritual', SIMPLY TO CARE. Questions, lessons, there are so many lessons for us all to learn. When we 'care', we radiate 'love', and love is the greatest power of all. Love can move mountains. Love for every living thing, our earth plane – our planet needs a lot of 'healing', a lot of love. Life on our planet (all things great and small), have suffered through man's selfishness, thoughtlessness, greed for wealth and power...we could go 'on and on'.

No matter in which age or generation of humanity we point to, the spirit, 'the real you', the real me, has always 'shone through'. It has shone through, out of the chaos, darkness, depravity, yes, even through a seemingly meltdown of humanity. A 'something' has always been there, to come to the rescue: perhaps in the wise words and actions of a beloved leader, the selflessness of so many who devote their time and energy to helping others, often in far-off countries where their very own lives are in danger. Workers all over the world who care about our planet and all life on it; or in the fun we have had in watching and listening to the world-famous Mohammed ALI, his 'strutting' around plus his confidence; 'It's hard to be humble when you are as great as I am' or;

'It's just a job. Grass grows, birds fly, waves pound the sand. I beat people up.'

Then the wisdom;

Mohammed Ali, humble, yet noble enough to say that he thanked his illness, Parkinson's disease, for it brought into his life a deeper understanding of suffering, a better awareness of the difficulties faced in everyday life by those that are less fortunate, and an empathy with his brothers and sisters all over the world. (His brothers and sisters all over the world says it all, don't you think!)

★

'I have had, especially during my childhood, several experiences where I felt very strongly that a power in which I could be wholly confident was acting for and around me, even if at that time I was too little to give it a divine explanation.'

Those words, under the heading 'Spiritual Feeling in a Scientific Age', written by Professor Alister Hardy, F.R.S. sum up perfectly what I have been trying to express in the previous pages. He tells us that over the years, his colleagues and himself, have collected together over four thousand 'first hand' accounts which show that 'even people today possess A DEEP AWARENESS of a benevolent non-physical power; many people having deeply felt "transcendental" experiences which have made them aware of the presence of the power.' He continues, 'They do not necessarily CALL IT A RELIGIOUS FEELING', and it usually induces in the person concerned a conviction that THE EVERYDAY WORLD is not the whole of reality; that there is another dimension to life.'

That the everyday world is not the whole of reality …Jacquie expressed it in her experience with the swinging light bulb; John as he stood in the middle of Flodden Field, the scene of the horrific battle fought there all those years ago, and Joe, who gave a prediction to his teacher when in his teens, which turned out to be true.

We never forget these, perhaps seemingly small, experiences. 'They are All Important' in the fact that they can open a window, 'even if it is only a tiny crack'. Give us a glimpse of a 'something else', a deep awareness that 'yes', it is there, for real, 'another dimension to life'. We remember, perhaps with a feeling of 'comfort, 'warmth', and the knowledge that 'yes' there really is 'something out there in the Universe to believe in'.

It is something to believe in, and to turn to, when we hit the rough times, the hard times, the bad times that we can all experience; often called, the lessons of life; and in the words of President Obama in his book *The Audacity of Hope* – that we are not just destined to travel down a long highway toward nothingness.

★

John Lennon and Yoko Ono were in Athens. They were about to go on a trip around the Greek Islands on a yacht owned by the singer Donovan (this was in November 1969, two months after he had secretly left the Beatles).

Wandering around the streets of Athens, quietly enjoying the sights, they visited an astrologer who gave John the 'startling', shocking prediction, that he would be 'shot' on an island.

So worried and alarmed by this prediction were they that they cancelled the trip; John and Yoko assuming the shooting would be on a Greek island. The assassination did happen, eleven years later. John was 'shot dead' by Mark Chapman on December 8th. 1980 as he returned to his apartment building on Manhattan island, New York.

In the year 2000, Yoko Ono, interviewed by the 'film maker' Nico Mastorakis, who filmed the couple wandering the streets of Athens at the time, recalling the visit to the astrologer said: "I totally believe that some people are psychic and that the message comes through some people. In our case, we were not careful in the way we should have been. We were careful but in the wrong way as we did not go to the Greek islands."

And so, where do we go from there, a prediction made true eleven years later, and it must have been hard to live with if you took it seriously, which I feel sure both of them did. We are talking, yet again, about 'fate', that tantalising subject that could drive you crazy if you let it; that we may argue about forever more, and never satisfactorily resolve. Perhaps the best way of looking at fate is to accept that, 'yes', it is there for each one of us. Perhaps it is that the broad outline of a life is laid out, such as when we are born; some of the big decisions we make such as 'marriage', and what I personally feel sure about (but I don't *know,* of course), is when we take our transition, pass away – die! 'Fate', yes, that is *the* big question.

Fate, but, thinking again, *is* it the big question? Can we reassure ourselves, remember that, as already touched on, we all of us experience something, no matter how small or seemingly insignificant in life, that does make us stop for a while, stop for a while, and ponder. And however 'small', *however small,* the experience might appear to be at the time, can take on a bigger 'presence' than we at first thought it deserved as it insists in occupying a bigger 'space' at the back of our mind. Becoming one of those small – experiences – we perhaps do not quite understand, and we find ourselves saying, 'Well, I don't believe in anything …but there was – one – thing…' There will always be a 'one thing,' a 'something', to help us along the way on our road through life but will we understand it when it comes; will we 'get the message', that is another big question.

Messages can come in as many different ways as there are grains of sand. The Bible even reassures us that if we forget, or perhaps fail to understand a message (remembering that an Angel is one of God's 'Special Messengers'), the message will be repeated to the angel time and again to deliver, hoping that, finally, it will be received, and understood.

(*There is a greater interest and belief in Angels now, in our present scientific age, than we realise.)

Bible stories and truths being accepted now as sacrosanct; scientists having proved that even the seemingly 'far-fetched' ones as being possible, for example, the story of the parting of the Red Sea, one of the most dramatic episodes in the Old Testament, when Moses and the Israelites are trapped between Pharaoh's advancing chariots and a wall of water. Thanks to 'divine intervention', a mighty east wind blows all night, splitting the waters to leave a passage of dry land with walls of water on both sides. The Israelites then make their escape. New research has shown that this could well have happened with freak weather conditions – a powerful wind could have divided the waters just as depicted in the Bible.

The Bible stories are full of messages, revelations being 'delivered' by angels; stories we loved, known from childhood; the annunciation, announcement by the angel Gabriel to the Virgin Mary, the message of the birth of Jesus, and that she was to be the Mother of God. The wise men alerted to 'following the star' as they made their way to find the place where the baby lay. Joseph instructed, again in a dream, to take Mary and the baby Jesus away quickly to safety, before King Herod discovered where they were. We are familiar with these wonderful stories but have we noted just how often it is through 'messages' that they are given, and 'played out'.

Guidance, messages, were available to the first humans through studying the sun, the moon, the stars, the whole of the universe – and is the saying 'put it out to the universe', not in vogue today? It is as usual to hear that bit of 'advice' for an answer to whatever, 'put it out to the universe', as it is to hear what is, the same thing, 'pray about it'. Every one of us has, or will, at some 'worrying' time in life, needed help, advice, comfort, and when we ask with sincerity, we 'will be heard'. (We should not forget to give thanks for the 'divine intervention' we will surely receive.)

Even a donkey used to force Balaam, a figure from the Old Testament, onto a different pathway in order to fulfil the word of God. Three times the donkey he was riding stopped on the journey and would not move; – confronted, as Balaam himself found out later, by an angel who insisted and forced him, the donkey, onto this different route. Balaam 'struck' the donkey each time to try to make him go on his (Balaam's) route but was finally 'humbled' and chastised by the angel for striking the donkey and ignoring the message; the journey continued and they got there in the end, Balaam no doubt, a sadder and a wiser man.

A conspiracy against Daniel – remember what was a well known saying – 'dare to be a Daniel' – landed him in trouble with the King who threatened and then commanded that he be thrown into a den of hungry lions; But the Lord God protected Daniel and, knowing this, Daniel knew no fear. On 'being released' into the 'den', the lions simply ignored him, lay down and went to sleep. By now the King, having regretted his decision, was relieved to find Daniel safe and well the following morning.

Marvellous, exciting stories from the Bible, still reckoned to be the most popular book of all time.

And the Bible is still in use today, yes, in our twenty-first century, by millions of people, and not only those who go to church. It is a strong symbol of wisdom and strength even for the many who profess to be 'non-believers'.

An 'almost completely' destroyed Bible 'was saved' from the ruins of the Twin Towers attack on September 11th, 2001. In the attack, the badly charred remains were 'fused' together on to a piece of *'heart shaped steel'*. The heart shape of the 'steel' was due entirely to the terrible destruction and exactly as it was when dug out from the wreckage by a 'fireman'. The fireman gave it to a photographer who had been working in the ruins for two years. They were both 'overcome', awed, by the find, especially as the message of God was still visible IN ONLY TWO VERSES that were left intact and readable, although the rest of it was badly singed, flaking – burnt out, as it lay, 'fused' on to this 'heart of steel'.

"The two verses are of great importance," as the photographer pointed out, "for the future of mankind if we are to survive, and take our world safely through the potentially calamitous times we now find ourselves in."

The verses are from Matthew chapter 5, verses 38 and 39.

> 38 Ye have heard that it hath been said, 'An eye for an eye and a tooth for a tooth';
> 39 But I say unto you, that you resist not evil; but whosoever shall smite thee on thy right cheek, turn to him the other also.

The meaning apparently is to love everyone, and not just those who love you. It is easy to love those who love you – but to love even those who would persecute you; to try to have love and understanding for all.

To think that this Bible has survived a 'millennia', though scorched and fragile as it now is with only two verses readable; two verses that could not be more 'significant', relevant, and that *are* surely a message for the world, badly needed in our dangerous, chaotic times.

The photographer wrapped the Bible carefully, lovingly, reverentially in his scarf, both himself and the 'fireman' over-awed at the find and especially marvelling at the two verses.

After a few years of wondering as to where best to place it, finally he decided to take it to the Ground Zero, September 11th Memorial Museum; and he hopes that the people who look at it will see it with the same wonder and awe that he, and the fireman did, seeing it as a miraculous story of 'survival' with a message, a message for the world.

There are many people, including myself, who still turn to the Bible for a message, not only to be comforted, reassured, but if puzzled or anxious, or worried perhaps about what to do in a certain situation.

To receive your own message, sit quietly, holding the Bible closed having taken out any bookmarks, holy pictures, memorabilia; simply hold the Bible, say a prayer – (send out a thought), asking for guidance and so on. As already mentioned, it is only when this is done in sincerity that you will receive. Without looking, open the Bible at random and note the words where your eyes first 'alight', holding them in your gaze until you understand the meaning. A good idea is to have pen and paper handy and write down the number of the chapter and verse so that you always have it to refer too.

One of the best messages I ever received was when going through an extremely sad, worrying time, and in a sombre mood of prayer, I pulled a tiny scroll from a special box with the words 'The darkest hour is just before the dawn.' How true those words proved to be and for which I will be forever grateful.

Intuition, coincidence, a missed phone call leading to a change of plan leading to…perhaps missing a flight; unexpected meetings, dreams; winning the 'jackpot' the best thing that could have ever happened to you until you realised that it was the worst! An advert setting in motion thoughts and actions that led to an unbelievable change in circumstances, a lost letter, a misunderstanding, a silly 'row', a kind act. All found in life's box of surprises, often urging us on to better things, sometimes holding us back from the not so good, but oh how the messages are always there for us and we do often have a straightforward sense of 'knowing'! However, do we take notice? That is another story.

Clare Hollingworth took notice. She took notice of her sense of 'knowing' which spoke to her through her 'heart'. 'My heart told me I must do this,' she explained, as she told her marvellous life stories, experiences as a war correspondent, and this until a 'senior' age. Living until she was one hundred and five years, she described her life when she was 'very elderly' as feeling like being eighteen years of age, but it was her body that let her down.

In Poland in the year leading up to the start of the Second World War, she saved thousands of lives in her determination to bypass slow and often reluctant government officials, earning herself the nickname 'the Scarlet Pimpernel' from the British press. Called home, perhaps because of her unorthodox methods and determination to save the refugees, it was only one month later when she was appointed as a war correspondent for the *Telegraph*, returning to the Polish – German border where she stayed with a diplomatic friend from the foreign office.

Now, in this story, are we into 'fate' again, in a 'big-way'?

Driving alone along the border, feeling safe as she had a diplomatic flag displayed on the car, a fabric partition separating the two countries 'flapped' in the wind, exposing scores if not hundreds of tanks in the valley below.

Three days later, at 5 a.m. on September 1st 1939, she was

awoken by the sound of tanks rolling past her window. Rushing to call her editor and the Polish and British Offices, each of whom viewed her news with disbelief (Poland thought that it was still in negotiations with Germany), she broke the news that World War II had started. It was the paper's greatest scoop, the scoop of the century.

★

In the small old seaport town of Blyth, situated in the North East of England, in the summer of 1938 and in the grim, dark days leading up to the start of the Second World War, a miraculous happening occurred. It happened in a ground-floor flat, part of a short terrace of old houses near the docks, and centred round a baby girl of two months, Norah.

Blyth was a place where, as perhaps with most other places in England at that time, poverty was the norm, and no one felt safe, especially Norah, the mother of baby Norah and 'two' young sons. Norah called her baby 'the miracle baby' as she weighed only four pounds at birth and had developed serious chest problems.

Her husband John, known as Jack, was a merchant seaman and at sea with no idea as to when he would return. Jack was later one of the lucky ones to 'be rescued' from Dunkirk.

A priest had called during the day and so worried was he by the baby's condition that he went immediately to seek a doctor.

That night, with the cot standing tightly pressed against the side of the bed, Norah half-lay, numb with anxiety, propped up on one side by her elbow, looking for any movement, any sign of life in a baby lying so still in her cot, the difficulty, the strain of breathing, sapping her already weakened strength.

It was then that the incredible happened. Suddenly the room was 'charged' with an extraordinarily beautiful perfume, strong yet soothing. Not recognised by Norah as being from this world... leading into further disbelief, astonishment, as, by now, 'mesmerised', she gazed on two Angels – who – 'just appeared', with sweeping wings widespread flying over the cot, and as suddenly disappeared… while the baby's breathing steadied; she was peaceful; she was 'well'. Norah, the miracle baby, grew up to become a popular and much respected nurse, and a mother of three.

Angels fly… time passes… pages turn.
big ships little ships small boats any boats
Unprepared for war, we the people of Britain were in a 'totally' desperate situation.
The Nation 'is called' to prayer.
The Nation Prayed.
big ships little ships small boats any boats

The German High Command boasted that The British Army 'is encircled and our troops are proceeding to its annihilation'.
Miracle of miracles Hitler stopped his general advance.
Big ships little ships small boats any boats while the sea, the English Channel, remained as calm as a milk pond when thousands of men of the British Army were rescued from Dunkirk.
Big ships——All ships, forever and affectionately, known as; 'The Little Ships of Dunkirk'.

★

Now we move on to the Second Chapter and other Miracles of the Second World War.

My Presence shall go with Thee

'Hugh Dowding's fight started long before there appeared to be any serious threat of another war on the horizon in thirties England. Throughout his years of service in the air force, he had a complete commitment to its success. Through his relentless pressure on his staff and superiors, committees, anyone or anything that hindered whatever he believed was the correct course to take, even to, much later on in his career, the government; his determination to be the best and to do the best for his country, and therefore for any staff serving under his command, was total.

During the First World War, serving both as a soldier then a pilot, the following anecdote is perhaps an early example of 'what was to come'.

★

Flying from Farnborough for Bruges to support a ground force attempt to relieve Antwerp, the observations of Germans the object, "no Germans were seen", he reported. "No Germans were seen, but owing to the difficulty of observation I cannot say that we did not pass any. Then the motor failed and the machine was broken in a failed landing!"

Dowding made his report, filed it, and was then 'summoned' to the headquarters of General Sir Henry Rawlinson who was responsible for that section of the war front.

General Rawlinson: "You say you saw no Germans, but they're there; we know that they're there."

Dowding, unimpressed, replied: "Well sir, you wouldn't wish me to say I'd seen them if I hadn't. It was a very clear day and if there had been any Germans, I must have seen them."

He 'was not invited' to stay for tea'.

From my innermost being I sense the endless scheme of things
But in the evidence of now, there is You and I.

CHAPTER TWO

AND SO IT WAS

Sept 8th 1940

His Majesty, King George VI, and Parliament, called for another National Day of Prayer, the second one in four months. The Nation responded.

With sirens blaring and screeching, the horrors of bombing imminent yet unpredictable; food stocks lower by the day and our merchant ships not able to return home safely, with shortages of all necessities at danger point, we now faced immediate invasion. It had to happen, it was there – on our doorstep; but the country held on; 'pulled together', prayed. The Nation united, were as one.

For the past two months, the German air force, the Luftwaffe, had targeted RAF airfields and radar stations in preparation for the invasion but, astonishingly, amazingly, the invasion plans were 'put on hold'. Hitler decided to destroy London first, to annihilate the most famous city in the world, conquering, demoralizing the citizens, and so forcing England to surrender.

Terrifyingly, air attack after attack started. 348 German bombers escorted by 617 fighters 'stormed their way' across London, the fires they ignited guiding the second wave of attacks that continued until 4.30 the following morning, Sunday, the 8th of September, 1940.

This was the beginning of the Blitz.

The beginning of the Blitz and a period of merciless bombing on London and other cities that continued until the following May. 'For 57 days London was bombed by day and by night.'

May Pearce was just one young ambulance driver whose nerve wracking experiences in the horrors of the London Blitz reflected every other person's experience of the Blitz, whatever they were called to do. She was in an ambulance forced to move slower than slow on chaotic streets and by-roads. Amid smoking ruins, buildings collapsed or about to collapse, confusion reigned. People now unrecognisable in their 'sameness' of dirt-ragged clothes, 'blackened' faces, and with cobwebs of wispy smoke clinging as haloes on tired heads helter-skeltered everywhere. Life was unreal.

With the ambulance often at a standstill, May was quick to help wherever she found herself, joining the rescuers, the passers-by, the residents working hour after hour in still-hot ruins pushing, pulling, lifting, doing whatever and however they could to reach the trapped, the injured, the dying, and those already too late to save.

Miracles did happen and a little girl of five was one of them. Blasted out of her bed on the first floor of her home, she was 'catapulted' through a window, shattering the glass as she flew into the night air to land safely, shocked but unhurt, in a garden. Sightings of 'angels in the sky' (some perhaps visible through cloud formations) were frequent and other signs of help emanating from an 'other worldly presence' were in evidence.

The people prayed. The government, leaders, generals, officers, the magnificent courageous lads and lasses of our armed forces prayed.

We were truly a country 'in dire straights'. With our

'Overwhelming Victory' in the Battle of Britain still to come and the miracle of St Paul's. At this point in our reflections on the Second World War, can we interrupt our thoughts and try to 'take in' the tremendous debt we owe to that same airman who, during his time in the First World War, 'was not invited to stay for tea'.

It was to Hugh Dowding, who became AIR Chief Marshal Dowding, and to his brave pilots, many who were young and inexperienced, that Prime Minister Winston Churchill was referring on leaving after a visit to the Operations Room, RAF Command Headquarters, during a day battle. Visibly upset, choked with emotion, he turned to Major General Hastings Ismay saying, 'Don't speak to me, I have never been so moved.' Then, after a few moments of silence, he said, 'Never in the history of mankind has so much been owed to so few,' the words forming the basis of his speech to the House of Commons on 20th August, after the Battle of Britain. The commander of 'the few' was Hugh Dowding.

Air Chief Marshal Dowding had known for a long time, since the beginning of the First World War, the great need, the urgency, there was in the country for a strong, 'well equipped', 'well-trained' air force. It was to this 'need', this urgency, that he gave all his strength, all his commitment, as a result of which, he changed the course of history, preserving life as we knew it, preventing the further rise of a depraved, self-ambitious, cruel and ruthless dictator.

Air Chief Marshal Hugh Dowding was a great believer in the other side of life, the spirit world. He wrote books about it and was a regular communicator, through prayer, with this other side. He was always ready to recognise the help that we received from these 'Invisible Sources', spirit.

Always a conscientious, serious-minded man, he was given the nickname 'Stuffy', but there were many who knew him well and who spoke out against that name, including Patrick Huskinson, who became one of the RAF's ablest masters of air armament problems despite being blinded in an air raid in 1941. He served under Dowding at this time and has written about him.

'Tall and wiry, a tireless worker and a ruthless driver, his cold and somewhat intimidating manner, which earned him the nickname "Stuffy", hid the gentlest, the kindest and the most generous of natures.' Patrick Huskinson continues, 'I could not have wished to be in better hands.' Huskinson also thought that it was a 'national blessing' that Dowding became head of 'Fighter Command', but he also praised his vital role in, what was at that time, the 'unspectacular organisation of air force training…' for which Dowding fought so vehemently, and gave so much.

Author Vincent Orange, in his fascinating book on Dowding entitled, *Dowding of Fighter Command, Victor of the Battle of Britain* has the heading 'Round One' on the top paragraph of Chapter One, 'Round Two' in Chapter Eleven, and 'Round Three' in Chapter Seventeen. Words not written in any gimmicky, light-hearted way but with all the solemnity and seriousness of mind he could muster in his writing when referring to the 'fights', the struggles, the overwhelming obstacles Dowding had to battle throughout his service to put forward the pitfalls, the plight, of our air force. Neglected, pushed to one side as it was, *our many young and inexperienced pilots with little and poor training going out there in old, under equipped planes,* he was heart-broken at the thought and all this RIGHT AT THE TIME when he knew it would face, it would *have* to be, the 'centre piece' of the combats to come.

Without an investment in new planes, without a strong, well-equipped, well-trained air force, Dowding knew we would face catastrophic defeat, absolute catastrophic defeat. He found the heavy casualties suffered by all the Allied squadrons hard to bear or to understand. Sholto Douglas, an officer with whom he would later have many disagreements, wrote that Dowding had 'a concern more heartfelt' over casualties than any other commander and he never changed in that regard. Many years later, another officer remembered him (Dowding), saying, 'People talk very lightly about casualties. They'll say, we only lost four pilots today. I feel as if I had lost four sons.'

He was a very serious- minded man, known for his humility and great sincerity, one who cared for his men and always had their best interests at heart. Unwilling to sacrifice pilots and aircraft, this very spiritual man, far from being old 'Stuffy', set out to learn from his men about any faults that could be 'corrected' in the aircraft and their operation. In his talks to them, he would gather groups around him, encouraging them to speak out frankly, listening carefully, noting every suggestion; and as he stood and watched the young, eager faces, ready and willing to make the ultimate sacrifice for their country, he later wrote a message to them all, beginning:

My dear fighter boys,

I don't send out many congratulatory letters and signals, but I feel that I must take this occasion, to tell you how proud I am of you and the way you have fought since the 'blitzkrieg' started. I wish I could have spent my time visiting you and hearing your accounts of the fighting, but I have occupied myself working for you in other ways. I want you to know that my thoughts are always with you, and that it is you and your fighting spirit that will crack the morale of the German Air Force and preserve our country through the 'trials' which yet lie ahead. Good luck to you.

A young WAAF leaving the office building in the early hours of the morning after work, passed Dowding who had been working late in his office after a full day, and noticed how haggard and exhausted he looked. 'His face grey with fatigue, yet still giving her a smart salute as he said goodnight, making time to be polite and caring towards her as he held the door open until she passed through.' Writer Wykenham, himself an air marshal, tells us that Dowding carried heavier burdens than most of us can even imagine.

Apart from constant worry over pilots and aircraft and being thwarted at nearly every turn. Constantly questioned, 'pilloried' both politically and personally by powerful men, he bravely continued to put forward and fight for his beliefs, even to taking on the government, as I mentioned at the start of this chapter. Until – until, after a long, wearisome and often bitter struggle (and possibly because of the sheer desperation of our situation), he was backed by Prime Minister Churchill who 'believed in him' and thought him a genius.

Churchill gives us another glimpse of the depth of thought and planning Dowding displayed when right from his involvement in the First World War, he saw the great need there was for major planning and organisation never before even visualised. On a visit to Group Headquarters, Uxbridge, 'Churchill's words', 'my wife and I were taken down to the bomb-proof Operations Room, fifty feet below ground. All the ascendency of the Hurricanes and Spitfires would have been fruitless but for this system of underground control centres and telephone cables which had been devised and built before the war by the Air Ministry, under Dowding's advice and impulse.'

His achievements in the following months that gave us our spectacular, unbelievable success, were a result of his long years of work and worry, and as he always acknowledged, 'help', from 'Invisible Sources', the other side of life.

Refusing to send planes to France – who had already capitulated to the Germans; if we were to fight on, we needed every single one of our already depleted 'force' based here.

The Air Ministry's opinion of the 'minimum strength' to do so was fifty-two squadrons. We only had thirty-six on hand. By reply, he sent a letter to the Air Ministry that has become the most famous letter written by any 'airman' at any time in any country to any recipient.

> *'If an adequate fighter force is kept in this country, if the fleet remains in being, and if home forces are suitably organized to resist invasion, we should be able to carry on the war single-handed for some time, if not indefinitely. But if the 'home defence is drained away in desperate attempts to remedy the situation in France, defeat in France will involve the final, complete and irremediable defeat of this country.'*

The framed original now hangs in an honoured place in the RAF College at Cranwell in Lincolnshire.

Churchill ruled on 19th May 'that no more fighter squadrons were to leave Britain, no matter how serious the situation became in France'.

Dowding achieved his brilliant success by:
- Refusing to allow planes to 'be sent' to France:
- Re-establishing the command of the air force; giving it independence throughout therefore 'opening the door for massive changes', the heady improvements that had to take place so strengthening Fighter Command.
- Better and longer, more in-depth training for pilots:
- New Planes, the Hurricane and the Spitfire; fully equipped with weapons, servicing, suitable runways, operations rooms, and all staffed appropriately.
- Radar; the development of which he knew was the key to success.

He oversaw the planning and preparation of all these measures every step of the way and, of course, insisting on the development of RADAR, bringing in better communications all round, he was so worried that pilots could not find their targets.

During a training session, a night exercise set-up for them in 1937, two-thirds of a bomber force failed to find the very large and fully illuminated city of Birmingham. Matters did not improve; during 1938 and thirty-nine numerous bomber crews simply got lost.

It was determinate, 'well planned', 'well targeted' bombing that ensured almost absolute success in the German assault on the City of London.

Sunday, 29th December 1940 was the night of the most ferocious air attack on the City. It was the road to destruction, complete desolation, Hell. The city burned.

'The raid was timed to meet the (Thames) dead-low-water hour, with water mains broken and nearly fifteen hundred fires to be fought, the attack concentrated on the city itself. "A void of ruin at the very centre of the British World".'

With no water, fire stations were soon inoperable, people fleeing from one place to 'anywhere' to avoid the swiftly encroaching flames, with one street collapsing after another the situation soon became hopeless; a real moment of crisis. We were a nation in peril.

Churchill sent out orders, the message to firemen and any other helpers: 'St Paul's must be saved , it must be saved for the morale of the people.' It was our symbol of Hope! He knew that it was an essential sign to the people that we would survive.

Already eight Wren Churches 'were destroyed or badly damaged'.

Our beautiful historic centre, the city of London, so revered and loved, annihilated. In the dark night, the glare of fires stoking up into great flames dancing from one furnace to another and the smell of destruction signalled the end. A great city, finished, lain in waste, sticks and stones, heap after heap of rubble as far as the eye could see, great buildings demolished, gone. North, south, east, west the people, citizens, lost, deranged at the horror of it all, petrified with fright and with no end in sight.

Helpless, homeless, they simply stood staring into a great emptiness, a great black space of thick, acrid smoke now merged with the dark clouds of night. Staring into a great abyss ringed with huge flames of uncontrollable fire – but then, did they, suddenly, through the thick black smoke, was it possible, could they glimpse a shape; a tall dark shape, a familiar shape, a mark on the landscape that they believed lost, gone forever; could it be real?

It stood as if lonely; a tall, towering edifice set on a gentle rise of land taking it above the common – place, the ordinary, 'undisturbed'. Set in its own special presence, undisturbed by the chaos, the ugliness, the horror of sounds and scenes that only war can bring. ...Undisturbed, with something beautiful, 'ethereal', everlasting yet worldly engulfing its place, the symbol of hope for a heartbroken but not defeated nation and a great city.

This was the miracle of St Pauls.

'and so it was...'

★

'AND SO IT WAS', that with every new day, with every week and with every passing month, the officials, the forces, the government, the people, citizens of this great city grew in strength.

They grew in strength pulling together, looking out for each other with a kindness, a caring and a determination to put wrongs to right; to prove just what miracles can occur when standing together, praying together.

There is a continuing theme running through this story of The Second World War; the same theme recorded in every interpretation of events, from the words of the Prime Minister, Winston Churchill, to news reports, reviews, film, magazines, radio, in publicity from all around the world. This theme, repeated so admiringly, was that the nation acted as one; of the people, yes, a repetition of the same words, how they 'pulled together', and the fact that there was *never a shortage of volunteers', no matter what task befell.*

It was all very moving, very impressive.

Prayer days continued with churches packed and 'running over'. By May 10th/11th 1941, our 'Boys' (Air Chief Marshal Dowding's Boy's,) as he liked to call them, with their new training now behind them, and new planes fully equipped, well serviced, with radar and every 'backing' they could expect, saw off the enemy time and time again until the last night, May 10th/11th 1941, when it was estimated that over 3,000 people had lost their lives.

That was when the enemy left and did not return, with the war soon moving on to another theatre.

The war continued on the continent for a few more years but already the Germans must have been 'in wonder' at how their well thought out plans/campaigns were seemingly 'doomed' to failure – the weather 'suddenly changing', thus averting invasion (of yet another country). Enemy leaders becoming ill, one, having had a heart attack that left The German High Command in a complete state of confusion. As the war moved on another chief away on leave; faulty intelligence and a mistake in administration leaving troops without supplies of petrol just as an attack was about to begin.

Here, at home in England, National Prayer days continued to 'be called' by the King and the government and people flocked to churches all over the country. It was noted how remarkable things came about after these prayer days – as at the start of the war (never to forget the miracle of Dunkirk).

There were persistent reports of people seeing Angels in

the sky often after a prayer day, and the fact that some of these Angels were perhaps seen as the result of cloud formations does not detract from the fact that they were seen – Angels in the sky.

We had an unexpected Bumper Harvest in 1942 which was 'lucky' for us as food stocks were running low, the ships, our merchant ships used to bring food from overseas to our shores had to be taken for transportation of men and munitions to war zones.

R S Hudson, the Minister of Agriculture, in a broadcast after the BBC 9.00 o'clock news, said, 'Much hard work and technical skill have played their part in these mighty yields, amongst the richest of all time. But I believe that we have a higher power to thank as well, and from the depths of our hearts. Some power has wrought a miracle in the English harvest fields this summer, for in this, our year of greatest need, the land has given us bread in greater abundance than we have ever known before.'

Most of our generals and leaders, during the whole span of the war, knowing the seriousness of our circumstances also knew that we had nowhere else to turn for guidance and help other than to 'Almighty God', the popular expression used at that time 'for connecting'; Almighty God. Now, in our time, we might simply say a 'something' or, put it out to 'The Universe', 'Father, Mother God', but whatever the term we might use, we still, in our greatest need, turn to that 'something', and you know what – find that it works.

Did we, as a nation, thank God enough for our deliverance from an evil, that so easily could have been an evil destiny...it seems that we did.

Prayers of thanks were in full swing all over the country as our victory was 'celebrated' and after a special Thanksgiving service in St Margaret's, Westminster, returning to stand on the Balcony of Buckingham Palace, packed with Service Chiefs, the Prime Minister and members of the Cabinet. The Prime Minister,

Winston Churchill, spoke of always being aware of that guiding, guardian hand, then King George VI, who had, along with the government, called so many national prayer days, stepped quietly to the microphone, but with great emphasis in his voice, gave thanks to Almighty God.

In this 'mad crazy', 'crazy mad' world of 2021 in which we live, even the scientists are waking up afraid of what might have been invented or 'un-invented' while they were asleep; and ordinary people like you and me are sceptical of what news might greet us from one day to the next, while everything around us seems 'super real' or 'super charged' or something! So 'yes', as the old song says, 'The times, the times they are a-changin'. Better than that, they HAVE changed, dramatically.

However, there is one thing that will never change, that has been here since the beginning of 'everything', and I am daring to say that more and more of us are beginning to realise this. To know it, to feel it, and that is the fact that 'Number One', we are spirit here and now in a physical body (and not a physical body with a spirit).

It is 'our spirit' that rules our day, and this is a fact whether or not we believe it, whether or not we say our prayers or go to church.

'The mind is spirit, the brain is physical.'

Have you noticed, have you ever thought about how 'freely' the word 'spirit' is used in ordinary conversation to portray us? 'She has a good spirit, his spirit will see him through, '*they* have the right spirit to see *them* through'; how quick we are to say 'I'll send a thought (prayer) out for you when we hear a tale of trouble. 'I nearly jumped out of my skin', a good reminder that we *are* spirit, here and now.

Prime Minister Churchill, on walking around seeing and assessing bomb damage during the war, and worrying about health epidemics said,

'The power of enduring suffering in the ordinary people of every country when their Spirit is roused, seemed to me to have no bounds.'

We see it today with the plight of the refugees who, fleeing their homeland, ill, starving, devastated facing one tragedy after another yet still soldier on, turning to their faith, their 'inner' something, for help and guidance. The sight of a young Asian man half- kneeling, half standing at the side of a boat crammed with terrified people desperate, fleeing from torture and tyranny, his arms outstretched to the heavens, wide eyes staring upwards, calling out in prayer reminded me of the well known hymn:

'As o'er each continent and island, the dawn leads on another day, the voice of prayer is never silent...'

How true those words are now, today, even though churches are worrying about declining numbers and what they can do to 'stem the flow' so to speak. They are wondering about encouraging more 'charismatic' speakers into the services, and while the churches have that worry, how fascinating it is to see and hear just how many people's minds ARE opening to the spiritual side of life, how they have found their own way to that source of help and comfort. IT IS REAL, it is there, it has always been there, simply clouded over by the constant pull of the material (the world we live in).

*

Making their way through life, there are far more of us around who have a belief, an understanding, of the 'other side', than we realise; perhaps the difference being that now, such is society that we can talk openly, freely about such beliefs. Air Chief Marshal Dowding was 'castigated' for his long-held belief in the spirit world to the point of being 'sacked' and right at the time of the war. However he was 'reinstated' quite quickly and accepted his rather 'nasty' experience with a good heart, such was the worth of the man.

There is a greater understanding now of how the 'other side' might work, many of us understanding a sudden 'shiver', perhaps of excitement or dread, fear, some overwhelming feeling – with a message, and how to deal with the situation. There is a strong belief in Angels, perhaps our own Guardian Angel, or a spirit helper, to walk by our side.

Pamela misplaces things, we all do, but she has a small business and plays a big part in family life 'helping out' with grandchildren. It could be important papers that she has mislaid, but after she has hunted, searched, retraced her movements to the point that she can do no more, she sends her thoughts 'out to the Universe' asking for help, and as she says, is never disappointed.

Jenny had been visiting her mother who was ill in hospital. On leaving her, she was quite content in her mind that all was well. Five minutes later, as she reached her car, a sudden 'shiver' went right through the whole of her body and in that instant she knew she had to return to her mother, to find that she had 'passed away'.

Apparently, nurses have often remarked that it seems to be that there are patients who want to be alone when their time comes' and that they seem to 'hang on' until all company have left. During their training, nurses used to be told to 'be sure a window was left open near to a patient who was dying', to make it easier for the spirit to leave.

Can we now imagine, in our twenty-first century, just how horrific it must have been in the late 1930s and 40s, during the Second World War. Not really so long ago, perhaps in our parents' or grandparents' time, and they endured, suffered, and it seems without making too much of a 'fuss' but always remembering, and sharing, stories, incidents that were too important, too good to be lost in the jaws of time; great material for future books, films, sitcoms, such as:

Jane's family lived in Hayes, near EMI the record factory, (records and other goods). The Germans used to try to shoot the workers as they came out on a Saturday lunchtime and it was a bit 'scary' living so near. Her parents were going out together, 'courting', the common expression then, and her father was a policeman, 'on the beat' in London.

One Saturday, he phoned her mother at lunchtime to arrange a meeting for that evening. As she picked up the phone he was immediately put into a state of shock hearing rapid gun shots and her grandfather shouting, 'Get down,' grabbing the phone yelling, 'Ring you back'…a bullet had gone right through the wall where her mother was standing. But she couldn't ring back as Jane's father was calling from a public phone box, and would have to wait many hours to see if Jane's mother was OK.

A close shave.

★

Never to be forgotten encounters and I wonder how many people can remember the 'call to prayer' days. Communications were poor then, and there would have been many who simply 'did not get the message'. Whereas now, there is so much information to be had. I for one, recently read about people in the Second World War who could be simply walking along the street, just at the time when a building collapsed; immediately finding themselves scrambling through wreckage and rubble to help in the rescue of any trapped inside. Then, when bodies were found and placed in a vehicle of some sort – lucky if it was an ambulance that arrived on the scene – there was sometimes the gruesome task of 'matching body parts'; enough on that scenario.

Not seeming, or perhaps not wanting to remember life at the time of our 'Two Great Wars', is this partly due to the fact that not enough was taught about it or *is* taught about it… in school? Although, whoever we talk to and mention the name, Joan of Arc, the legendary but true story of 'The Maid of France', they remember, and faces often 'light up' at the thought. Is this because of the impossibility of the tale, a young woman in those far-off times leading a huge army to victory; a gentle, kind, God loving girl who had the 'so called' supernatural with her from the day she was born and proved it!

There are reams and reams of documents full of testimonies from people in every 'walk of life' who knew her, from her neighbours, to the 'highest in the land', and all written down, documented, at the time. Accounts from the military, the courts, The Royal Court; it is described as the most documented story in 'the world'. A story we have all loved to hear and will never forget – even if we do mix up some of the facts; and for this, the most miraculous of stories, we go back to another country, another war, another time; 1412.

GOD moves in a Mysterious Way
His Wonders to Unfold

CHAPTER THREE

We ignore the Spiritual as sleepers numb to reality in
their pursuit of dreams.

1412. FRANCE WAS IN a state of deep decline with the constant
threat of civil war. 'Unsettled' as it was, with powerful men in
both England and France constantly seeking to champion their
claim to the throne through inheritance of this 'weak', vulnerable
country. The troubles were later known as 'The Hundred Years
War', from 1337 to 1453.

Into this climate of sad, deep destruction – with so many
different political and religious opinions, with conflicts that seemed
to have no end, was born in 1412, Joan, Joan of Arc (who later
wanted to be known as Joan, the Maid of Orleans).

She was born in the picturesque village of Domremy, a
province of France, on the banks of the river Meuse, with, nearby,
the ruins of an old castle and surrounded by luxuriant woods of
oak and beech. Her father was not a poor man but he worked
hard for his living, renting a large farm on which he kept cattle
and sheep and grew corn. She had two older brothers, the family
working together as one, supporting each other and although
Joan did not go to school, her mother was her teacher. All her

lessons were 'learned' by heart. She could spin and help in the fields, sew and repeat 'Our Father' and other simple prayers. Before she was seven, Joan had learned to love and trust in God so truly that every day she tried to please and serve Him better.

'Before I was seven I had learned all a child needs to know – to be good.' (These are Joan's own words.)

She was a strong, happy, healthy child, singing at her work, pleased when a holiday came along and she could dance, and skip and play with her village friends. They played in the sunny fields or the shady woods. They loved to run around through the woods, hiding, chasing, picking flowers, weaving garlands and sometimes had a picnic of little cakes, eating and drinking in the glorious out-doors.

As much as Joan enjoyed being with her friends, they were all aware that she also craved the 'solitude', and no-one was surprised when she disappeared to say her prayers, in the church, or in the quietude of the woods, intense in her longing to be good.

The children 'loved' her, she was always so kind and gentle, and laughed (kindly) at her, so often, as she put it, 'talking to God'. Her little bare feet were never weary of running here and there to help anyone who was sad, or in trouble or any sick animal or bird. She loved all wild life and revelled in the companionship of the animals and birds in the woods; staying with her as she fell silent in 'thoughtful mood', perhaps leading to yet another 'talk with God'.

Although the village of Domremy was an idyllic place in which to live, it did not escape 'outbursts of fighting' between various factions, in the unsettling times experienced by the rest of France too. Children, as quick as they are to pick up and sense the worries and fears of the grown-ups, worried and took sides in the never-ending wars in their country.

The boys of Domremy had been fighting the boys of Maxey, the village across the river. Domremy was for the French King, but Maxey was proud to belong to Burgundy, the powerful Duke also making a claim as one more 'rightful heir' to the throne of France.

One battle between the boys, built up by determined noisy marching and singing along the way, was particularly fierce. In grim earnestness, with pouches full of stones and wielding heavy sticks, they tore into each other, both sides suffering badly bruised limbs and bloody faces. Joan watched them from a distance as they set off as if already in triumph. Not wanting to join the other 'girls' who tagged on along the way, when they returned, bruised and battered, she cried, then rushed to clean their wounds and help them in any way she could.

As the black clouds of war, forever 'threatening', hung over France continuously, with savage sporadic fighting bursting out from 'who would know where', the French soldiers seemed to lose heart. They fought as men doomed to failure, so losing ground.

Joan was very young when she helped her father to drive the cows into the courtyard of the old castle to save them from the Duke of Burgundy's soldiers; the whole village was threatened and once the enemy burned down a part of the church. Everyone knew that they might burn down the cottages and houses as well. The threat was always there, but Joan, young as she was, never felt afraid; she loved God and trusted Him with all her heart. Over the years, quietly getting on with her work helping in the fields, in the house, spinning wool and hemp and sewing so beautifully that she soon became known as the best needlewoman in the village.

It was another beautiful summer; peaceful, still, nature sparkling at its best; the threat of yet another breakout of fighting, among the many differing 'factions', for the moment anyway, far away. Joan was running through the fields where she had been helping, watching the sheep with her friends, running home to see if her mother needed her. She ran through the little cottage garden and was about to enter the cottage when she seemed to see a bright light shining between her and the village church; and out of the light, a soft voice called to her;

'Be good, pray often, for you must go into France.'

Then the light grew even brighter and she had a vision of Angel Hosts from Heaven; three times the message repeated, 'Be good, pray often, for you must go into France.'

The light faded; the vision disappeared; Joan stood perfectly still, entranced by it all. Everything around her was 'as it always was'; the cottage, the church, the fields, the hills, but inside, she felt she was not the same and could never be the same again… she knew she really did belong to God now. Joan was thirteen years old. Not able to read or write, yet she had seen many beautiful pictures of Angels, and knew the wonderful stories from the Bible; stories of men and women who had lived such Holy lives and who had died so bravely for Christ's sake.

Joan knew that these men and women were 'Saints'. Humble as she was, and not for one moment thinking of herself as ever doing anything so noble or brave; felt that in giving her life in service – 'I will allow nothing to come between myself and His service' – vowed in her heart to devote herself, body and soul to 'Him', Father God.

All that day, Joan lived out a mixture of emotions, a little of happiness, excitement, and fear, her fear being, what was the meaning of the words 'you must go into France'. She had no idea at all of the meaning of that part of the message but had enough faith and understanding to know that 'all would be revealed to her', in God's good time. She never told anyone of the vision, or the message, but acted on it as best she knew how and one way was to try even harder to be more unselfish than ever.

We 'are privileged' to know as much as we do of the life of Joan of Arc from the amazing testimonies given about her; kept safely for over 600 years and available for anyone with a true interest in her life and times to study. Simonin was only one of countless numbers who gave testimony to the pure love and goodness of Joan, later known as the 'little maid.' He told how as a young lad, sick and in pain, Joan begged to 'be allowed' to nurse him and how she crept in and out of his miserable little room like an angel of mercy. It seemed that no one had such a soft, soothing voice as Joan, or such a gentle touch; she was a natural nurse, always seeming to know what to do. 'She nursed sick children well again' and would cheerfully give up her bed for anyone destitute or needy and sleep on the floor'.

To the last day of his life, as an old man, Simonin never forgot the little nurse of his boyhood. A rough lad who worked in the fields giving, in his 'rough' way, long after she was dead but still with tears in his eyes, his simple testimony.

Time passed and as the words in the vision, 'You must go into France' continued to worry her', she was forever asking herself the question, 'Why would I want to go into France WHY'? Leave the home and family she loved, the friends, the woods, church, river all that she had known and revered since her birth.

Still not revealing anything of her vision, now a few years away, but constantly troubled in her mind about it; even all her praying and asking questions to Father God did not seem to soothe her until, as she reached the age of sixteen, things started to happen. Slowly, gradually, she 'interpreted' the message of having to go into France as definite work for her to do, and now it was about to be revealed to her.

Imagine the state of her mind. It must have been in complete turmoil, in disbelief, shock, perhaps despair as she 'took in' the enormity of it all. This, the message that she had so long waited to hear:

'Go into France; raise the siege of Orleans; crown the Dauphin, God will be your aid.'

She was only sixteen.

Once she understood and accepted that God would be with

her, telling herself that, after all, she was only an instrument in the plan, she was 'filled with His Spirit', and was endowed with a courage that would never fail. Her voices told her how to begin her mission, but she must have shuddered within herself when fully realising what lay before her.

The English were fast taking Orleans, the most important city still left to the Dauphin, hemming it in on every side. Orleans 'must be set free' so that the Dauphin could be lawfully crowned in Rheims Cathedral, thus bringing the people together against their enemies. Joan understood this and now the great significance of her task was clear but the questions, how and why remained.

If we did not already know the truth of her story, the story of Joan of Arc would read as an impossible piece of fiction. However, we do know that it is true from the massive collection of annals written at the time; from these annals have sprung pictures, books, films; the story of a young girl dressed in boy's clothes protected by armour riding at the head of a huge army, holding a banner.

As she rode, she was fearless and always urging them 'forward and on', and they too were fearless with her as their commander ready to jump to her every command. Yes, it reads as fiction, the whole story, but in battle after battle they won the day. This army, they loved her. Giving their all, finally raising the siege of Orleans, saving the people, seeing the Dauphin crowned (and in Rheims Cathedral). What a story, what an achievement, what a victory! Then the great rejoicing and celebrations followed.

Time passed and with more troubles and skirmishes to come we know that finally she was captured.

'The Burgundians pressed around her, blades and hands closing in, until at last she was pulled roughly from her saddle... Word spread quickly, with excited shouts and ribald laughter in the Burgundian and English camps.'

In her captivity, she suffered constant persecution; the horrors, torments facing her that she heroically endured in her determination to fulfil her mission from God; 'Inspired by a power beyond that of earth.'

Joan arrived in Rouen on Christmas Eve 1430, a prisoner awaiting her trial. A prisoner held in the most inhumane conditions and with only male jailors attending her, a set-up that lasted for the rest of her captivity, seven months.

Her trial started just after sunrise on the morning of February 21st 1431. The accusations against her (among other things) were of lying about her 'voices', of being a witch, a heretic, insulting God and risking the souls of the simple folk who had followed her. The list was long.

The Inquisition was led by Bishop Pierre Cauchon, with forty-two clerics of great distinction, of the utmost probity and scholarship, and they ruled over this 'great' trial of Joan the Maid, as they termed it.

She had no chance. The twists and turns, the ins and outs, the prayers, sermons, 'lectures' questioning, opinions, the seemingly endless on and on of the trial ran on, while at the same time there were delays when she was unwell...ILL...existing in the same brutal, inhuman conditions with only male warders for company. She had no chance. Her fate was finally sealed on the day of May 30th 1431.

The old market place and streets of Rouen were packed and the feeling of excitement generated by the crowds was palpable; they waited for Joan to emerge from her prison cell, then to be assisted onto the cart, the executioner's cart that trundled through the streets to the market place where a scaffold had been erected.

Three tiers of high seating were in place for the dignitaries and other special guests while the executioner made ready the stake. English soldiers held her slight figure as she was bound to the wooden stake placed high enough for the public to have a good view. 'Onto her shaven head, before she left the castle prison, they had forced a cap bearing the words "relapsed heretic, apostate, idolater".' She had to endure another sermon, more preaching, and yet again, a listing of her sins...

The fire burned, the smoke swirled, but still Joan's voice heard as she prayed. Incessantly. In the heat, the smoke now ever swirling into thickening black fumes now her screaming of the name 'Jesus. Jesus. Jesus'. She was only nineteen.

*On May 16th 1920 Joan of Arc was recognised as a Saint of the Roman Catholic Church.

★

Newbiggin by the Sea, on the North East coast, had just enjoyed a busy week and a successful 'Arts and Crafts' exhibition of local work. It was the last day or so of the exhibition, a quiet Sunday afternoon, when I made my way upstairs to a large room that held the Art Work, beautifully and imaginatively displayed. It was on my second round of viewing when I was 'suddenly accompanied' by a man, probably in his thirties, Simon.

Simon told me he was a 'local' and on the committee to promote local Arts and Crafts. He is a historian with an excellent degree but feeling disappointed at not being able to find suitable employment nearer home.

At first, I thought that his subdued tone and quiet manner was because of this disappointment, but soon realised there was a deeper reason.

As the conversation turned to my interest/work, writing about the 'other' side of life, the Spirit World, he jumped in as quickly as he could with, 'Oh I don't believe in anything like that (familiar words), but then, just as quickly changed to 'Will you tell me how, if there *is* a God, he lets innocent people suffer so much such as when they are attacked, viciously attacked,...murdered...?'

Quietly, intently, he waited for my response.

Thrown by the sudden sad turn in our conversation, at first

I felt at a loss as to how to answer. Here was a highly intelligent young man who was badly disturbed by something.

Then, just as suddenly as there had been a change in our conversation, I felt myself smoothly, calmly, answering.

'The person under any attack, or accident, can be 'lifted', raised, out of the physical body, unaware of the trauma they have suffered and kept safe until help is found, or they are taken away in their 'spirit body', to the other side of life; but no one is ever left alone; in distress, or needing help. There are Spirit people whose job it is to be a first response to any emergency.

The answer seemed to satisfy him, to 'lift a cloud', and then I discovered that he knew more than I had given him credit for about our 'subject' as he immediately told me of an incident he had witnessed in the old part of the local library. Making his way to the librarian's desk, she was sitting deeply engrossed in sorting through a pile of old books, just as he was walking by a long line of shelves full of books, two or three of them 'jumped' off a shelf onto the floor; no one else around, nothing anywhere near to disturb them.

I smiled and only hoped my few 'impromptu' words had helped him, noting to myself how we were left completely alone to have the 'deep' conversation we had, and that he so obviously needed, sending out my own 'thanks' to spirit, hoping I had served them well.

To quote the words of Mike Hallowell, a fellow writer, after going through a hard time, 'It's at times like these when we realise how lucky we are to have God.'... Yes.

★

A medium is someone who can communicate between our two worlds, this one, and the next, the world of spirit. Pat Corke is a medium who 'has been blessed' to know about the Spirit World since she was a child. Having served Spiritualist Churches as a visiting medium for years, her experiences have been countless and certainly varied but, as a mother of three sons (now grown up), she stresses how she has had to keep herself well and truly 'grounded' in this world, while at the same time always ready and willing to use her gift to help others.

Deep thinker that she is, Pat does not put herself into any particular category of thought, except that she is a 'searcher'; a searcher who is looking for the 'ins and outs of things'; looking at the 'how' and 'whys'. Trying to put it altogether for her 'real' search, which is for the 'truth'; looking for the truth about 'life'. Walking, and along with the walking goes the 'thinking', the questioning, and no doubt the prayers. 'A lonely way to be,' as she says, but the way she likes it.

Pat enjoys reading about science, astrology, philosophy, (metaphysics and star children). She lives at Tynemouth, another picturesque small town set on the north-east coast, further down from Newbiggin by the sea, where Simon, featured in the last story, lives.

Having set the scene, now to tell you the extraordinary tale of an experience that Pat had many years ago, and which she could never forget or understand until... but now I will attempt to repeat it to you, this fascinating experience, with all its mystery.

It was well after the Second World War, about fifteen years, sometime in the sixties, and out walking one day, Pat decided to make her way down to the beginning of the Tynemouth pier. Nearly there, she remembers a big old crane, and having to walk under it to get to the pier, and thinking about 'the tea', and what she would make for her three sons. (She stresses this as a pointer to the fact that she was 'very much focused on *this* world').

All alone, no one else to be seen anywhere, she started her walk along the pier and was near the end when suddenly, giving her such a shaking, from out of nowhere came a man's voice shouting hysterically calling out something in German; then there were other men's voices joining in again in German not only calling but shouting in the chaos but chaos of what, what, what? Distressing voices forsaken voices calling, calling. Pat was still walking, panic rising. What could she do but turn and hurry back along the pier? Then suddenly she STOPPED REALISING the voices were calling from a boat; a boat that was under the waves, under the sea, the voices calling from a boat under the sea.

Then, just for one moment, for one split second of time in a state of 'heightened awareness' she knew that she was down there with them that she had interrupted something and she too was in the boat way down with them in a boat under the waves under the sea.

'Petrifying'; to take one step in ordinary life, 'what could be more ordinary than thinking about the tea, then suddenly, this, whatever it was, happening.' (Pat's words.)

Slowly making her way home, trying to shake off her worried, panicky feeling, even deeper in thought than when she had first set out on her walk, she puzzled over it all continuously. One thing she did know, however, one thing she had soon made her mind over, was the fact that she 'would not', she *could not*, confide in anyone about this experience; she knew that they would immediately class her as 'mad'. She could not confide in anyone but had to try to accept it in her own mind as a different, dramatic but unexplainable experience...and certainly not go back along the pier...any pier!

It took a long time for her to accept it, which finally she did but still with no understanding of what it was all about no matter how hard she tried.

Pat kept her word and never did confide her story to anyone, until, one day, years' later one of those strange incidents occurred; could it be coincidence, serendipity, or could it be simply fate? She met up with a friend she had not seen for a long time and they were so pleased to see each other again that they soon arranged for Pat to visit Janice, her friend, at her home. Little did she know that she was on the way to having some of the answers to what had been at the back of her mind now for years; the mystery of Tynemouth Pier.

The day came and, of course, the talk between the two friends was incessant. Tom, her friend's son, a sailor, studying marine biology and geography, kept popping in and out of the room, but nobody noticed. During the course of the afternoon Pat must have felt it to be the right time at last to unburden herself, share with someone else the experience that still gave her shivers when she dwelt on it too deeply, an experience that had haunted her over all the years. Never doubting any of it for one moment, she did feel, however, she did wish she could have some answers, some explanation for what had happened.

As she talked to Janice, bringing in her tale slowly and carefully, Tom, in his busyness, going in and out of the room had picked up enough snippets of the story, to be intrigued by it, wanting to know more. With permission to join them, we can imagine his eyes almost popping, getting wider and wider as he took in the full impact of this weird tale. Speechless at first, as Pat ended the story of her 'adventure' his sheer amazement in it made him stutter out question after question then fly away into another room, soon returning with an armful of books and maps and papers full of diagrams, all part of his studies.

The table was now strewn with yet more maps, books, pen and paper at the ready, questions fired and answers taken down. Tom wanted to know her exact position on the walk as she made her way to the sea and the start of the pier. The old crane – 'yes, yes'; where exactly had she walked from the crane then made her way to the sea and the start of the pier…and then, where exactly had she stood when she heard the voices, the screaming, and knew about the 'boat' as she called it, under the sea.

It was now Pat's turn to be stunned. As she stood by his side, Tom explained to her – his hands moving swiftly in all directions from maps to books to papers, exactly where she had been on that outing, and for Pat, suddenly realising the enormity of it all, it was mind blowing.

Pat had talked about a boat; the boat was a submarine, and she was standing right by the place where there had been countless battles in both the First World War and the Second World War between the German navy and the British fleet.

Excitedly, Tom pointed out the area she had been in as near to 'Dogger Bank', sixty miles out to sea from the pier she had walked along... and 'exactly parallel' with the crane and the pier.

Dogger Bank is sixty miles out to sea from the pier and the longest sandbank in UK waters; an extensive, isolated shoal rising seventy feet higher than the surrounding sea floor and the scene of 'horrendous' warfare in the two World Wars. Both the English and the Germans suffered alike with wreckages from both sides reappearing from time to time. Horrendous is the term usually used for such warfare. Miles of shells from submarines litter the seabed, lines of them lying undisturbed; Tom, pointing it all out on his maps and diagrams, showed where some of the wreckages lay; and all were in line with where Pat had walked and stood and heard the voices and, for a split second of time, joined them. As she listened, and studied the marks on the maps and diagrams, in her mind, she remembers thinking, 'Bloody Hell!' (Not her language at all.)

It is easy to understand why Pat has never been able to forget her experience along Tynemouth pier and never felt able to talk about it until, as is said, the time was right. The time for meeting up with Tom the sailor who had all the answers and the documentation as 'proof'. The time was right for her to share her story knowing it was in good, understanding 'hands' and to be able to think about it in a 'different', more 'comfortable' way.

Pat rested well in her bed that night after the amazing revelations of Dogger Bank were made known to her. Meeting up with her friend had certainly closed a chapter in Pat's life, and in the process had cleared her mind; now free from anxiety over the whole affair, she was well and truly ready to move on to the next one…(the next chapter I mean).

In an old radio interview, given by a man who had been a young sailor in a torpedo war in the First World War, he talked about his terrifying experience, and seemed to be re-living it all, as real as if it was only a few years away.

'All around the submarine, below the sea, there were a mass of torpedoes, lines of them lying there, exploded, unexploded; at night time, there was a torpedo strike…suddenly it was pitch black, water rising, water rising in the passages, under the door, over the door, everywhere…it was terrifying!'

★

Life; and what it can throw up at us, every single one of us, at any time, any place. Those words remind me of a sad story involving a close friend of ours, Ian (a friend of my husband Peter and I), as the three of us, meeting accidentally, stood together talking in a supermarket in the Middle East.

Ian – and Janice his wife – were our friends over many years, but it was Ian's answer to the tragically sad circumstances that had overtaken them to try to be nonchalant about it, as he said, 'Well Mary, that's life.' Those words of Ian's, 'that's life', haunted me as I tried to make sense of their awful situation and other such situations happening somewhere, all the time.

Is it, is it really 'life' itself that causes havoc, mayhem, devastation, trauma, heart-break? Could it not be 'life', and what *we* do with it, to it, the human element in the equation that causes a lot of the upheaval, sadness and despair, or are we back again to 'fate'?

Looking back over your own life, what do you think about 'fate' and Ian's words 'that's life'. Could you have made better choices in certain situations, did you ignore opportunities that seemed to be there, waiting for you, and regret it later? Do you believe, as it appears that many of us – and the numbers are steadily growing – are starting to understand and believe (although church attendances are reckoned to be down) in the spiritual side of life? That we are first and foremost spirit here and now in a physical body and not a physical body with a spirit. Do you believe that we only need to send out a thought, a prayer, to connect with that spiritual side? The still small voice ever urging us on to the right decision, the correct path, the true way. 'Ask, and you shall receive.'

Church attendances are going down, but is it not a fact that many people are finding their own way to that 'higher side of life' we all need if we are to be totally 'rounded citizens'?

In trying to be 'fulfilled' human beings, we need that 'light', that 'guidance', that help found in understanding and acting on our spiritual side. Engaging with it and not only as we hear so often, when there is nowhere else to turn, such as (the lady bracing herself for an impending plane crash), 'I only had time for a quick prayer', but those who look at, say, a coincidence, as one example of *perhaps* having a special meaning, a message, and 'take notice'.

There is a belief that a coincidence is God's way of performing a miracle anonymously.

Coincidences, consequences, thoughts, feelings, premonitions, dreams, strong intuition.

Intuition has been proved one of the strongest links of all to aid us, when we learn to listen and follow it with confidence.

With the spirit, our spiritual side of life, recognising it, even if our understanding is in the early stages, we 'feel' the love, and, as Einstein, perhaps the greatest of the scientists, wrote in his last letter to his daughter – 'The most powerful force of all, that includes and governs all others, is "LOVE".'

The Bible itself has many references to the power of love.

'Many waters cannot quench Love neither can the floods drown it.'

Is it not that what is lacking, and has been for a long time now (and we are all guilty in one way or another), is our treatment of our planet, the air, the atmosphere, nature? There is, and has been for a long time a total lack of understanding, of caring and respect, with reckless high-handed usage in this 'throw-away' attitude of our modern world, believing it is all there for the taking, and it will go on and on and on... . The same applies to the many who may have never given a thought about having a true feeling of 'love' or respect for nature. Think of 'the whole of nature', our environment – the air, the atmosphere, the sky and all its wonders, night and day, creepy crawlies, all insect life. Scientists in studies of the spider and the mystery, the genius of how it weaves its web, have looked for answers to apply to our building programmes. A late night newspaper report; 'shock at the zoo' after chimpanzees use a branch as a ladder to go 'sight-seeing').

Saint Francis called the animal kingdom our 'brothers and sisters'. A cyclist stopped his ride on seeing a little dog, a spaniel, standing at the side of the road, distressed, licking a carrier bag. It was full of her dead puppies. As he bent down beside her, he saw her eyes; they were full of tears. The cyclist was one who stopped and cared, stepping forward, going out of his way to help the little dog. Later, in a comment about it, he said, 'I could not believe that anyone could be so devoid of humanity, to do something like this.'

In an article in *The Sunday Times* October 2016, a good description of where we are in our world today had the heading 'Driven to Distraction'.

'We are the goldfish generation. Digital addiction is shrinking our memories and eroding our attention span. Fears are growing that unless we learn to unplug now, we will become the slaves of technology.'

Sadly, I must add to the 'goldfish' comparison another truth; 'Fish can feel pain.'

Have you noticed that we appear to be being side-lined as Christians in our own country? This thought has nagged away at me for some time now and is growing stronger with more evidence appearing, especially over the recent Christmas time of 2018.

'Side-tracked', 'side-lined', whatever you want to call it, by the government, the media, internet...the powers that be, it is happening and there are a good number of people out there who agree with me.

Over Christmas, with little or no mention of the Christmas story, the traditional one, according to one reporter in a national newspaper, we had: 'A Feast of the Material and Ignoring of the Spiritual.'

Recently, I listened to a radio programme by the experts on 'how to be happy'. This might have been a follow-up to the recent findings and the worrying state of the high number of people, young and old, with mental health problems. Listening carefully, I think that every possible cure was suggested except the Spiritual.

A new study has found that children who were in the scouts or guides were less inclined to suffer from mental health issues in later life.

It seems that many schools are reluctant to put on a nativity play, again, a true, traditional one, instead, making it into a comedy or performing it in the local dialect, deviations to which the young people themselves have objected.

Nowadays, with few Sunday Schools and little, if any, mention of the Bible in school assemblies – or even on the curriculum, where will our young people receive any religious education? Where will they hear those great stories from the Bible – while at the same time scientists are proving every day that the seemingly impossible stories (such as the parting of the Red Sea in the Old Testament), did happen.

How many parents (now) say to their children at bedtime, 'Don't forget to say your prayers,' which was a must not so long ago.

Still with Christmas 2018 so now to mention the tale of the Christmas stamps, or lack of them, with Post Offices refusing them to customers, for a variety of reasons:

'They are not being issued now; we haven't any left, there were only a small number issued. People are not interested in them. They are not popular with their dull, old-fashioned designs. They are boring and finished, the Post Office is not issuing any more.'

On insistence by customers for the shop assistant to please have a look to see if by chance there were any left lying around, assistants were *more* than reluctant to do this, insisting that there were none.

The *Telegraph* newspaper took up the issue and it was interesting to hear one of their reporters on a late night news programme relating the difficulties he had in trying to buy Christmas stamps and the excuses made for their unavailability.

A few pages ago, we were thinking about 'life' and what it can throw up at us as we travel along this 'highway', even if we don't travel very far.

I love all animals and could not bear the thought of their suffering, particularly through man's cruelty, neglect and of course feeding them up, etc, for consumption. My alternative was to become a vegetarian. As I did not like cheese, salads and other things on offer for a vegetarian, I was a hopeless case even to try. I fought against it, becoming a vegetarian for years... for a *long* time. While living in South Africa, life must have caught up with me because in one week three awful things happened to make me change and honestly, it really was not too difficult after all, and I have never looked back. I would like to tell you about the third thing that happened during that week, very sad, but not as horrendous as – but never mind here is the third 'experience' in that week that made me change.

I was teaching at a school in Johannesburg. The staff were warm and friendly and I looked forward to our conversations during break times, on this week especially as they were full of talk and plans for their annual fair day, hoping for crowds of visitors to boost the school funds; funds which were always needed.

On this particular day, Marsha, one of the teaching staff I was particularly friendly with, made her way across the room to sit beside me, and I could see immediately that she was not her usual controlled self. Within a few minutes, she whispered, 'Could we go somewhere quiet where we can talk?' which we did.

She had been asked by the head teacher, to go with one of the male teachers, to the local abattoir, and pick up parcels of meat they donated every year to the school for the Broth made by the staff…a best seller!

Marsha had done this before and so she was not too worried about it (going to the abattoir). They simply stood at the entrance and the meat was brought out, well packed, put in the car, no problem; but this year was different.

She faced a long line of little donkeys (a natural instinct probably telling them what was about to happen) afraid – yet patiently waiting their turn to go in through the big open doors.

(I am pleased that I have now finished writing the above, it will always hurt to think about it)

★

The government have made it known that plans are being worked on to encourage us all to become Vegan, or Vegetarian. This is for health reasons but also and perhaps mainly, for the preservation of our planet. Little did I think that I would ever hear such an announcement, remembering my worry over having to tell my family and in-laws about my change in preparation for our return home to England. It was not easy.

After a fair bit of 'gloom' and sadness in this chapter (I'm thinking mainly about the animals), but let's just blame the Christmas Stamps and the question 'are we being side-lined' as Christians in our own country...can we end on a happier note which is really what living in and with Spirit is all about.

At the top of the page at the start of each chapter in my last book, *The Reality of the Unbelievable*, I had a short experience, funny, amusing, but always true. I wonder if perhaps you missed reading them and you might like to do so now, I have picked out three.

Thomas, age five, chatted away as usual to what his mother called his 'imaginary friends'. Yet she stopped short in her tracks as, passing the open door to the living room where he was sitting, alone, legs astride, rolling a ball across the carpet, she was just in time to see it rolled back!

Grandma Norah was quite startled when her three and a half year old grand-daughter Grace, who is obviously learning a lot at her nursery school, asked her, 'Do you know Jesus? Norah (after a long, thoughtful pause) answered, 'Yes,' then waited for a reply. She waited and waited; another long pause, then Grace finally answered. 'He died.' A few weeks later she informed Norah, 'He is alive again now.'

Mrs Lambert was a strict but caring woman, always having to dress nicely, always clean and tidy, with everything in place. She was the mother of seven children, grown up by now and living away from home. They all possessed, as did Mrs. Lambert, 'the gift', also known as 'second sight'. Her husband, Joel Lambert (given as Joe for short), long since dead, had been a soldier in the First World War, and her proudest possession was a photograph of him in his army uniform. About to start cleaning and decorating, which she did herself, to keep the photograph safe, she put it inside a cupboard, hanging it up inside on the cupboard door, but turning it round so that it faced the door...(if you know what I mean). Margaret, one of her daughters, lived twenty miles away, on the other side of the river, and knowing nothing at all about her mother's cleaning and decorating escapade, was *more* than amazed when her dead father appeared to her, asking, 'Why has your mother put me in the cupboard?!'

Finally, as a meaningful little 'thought for the day', a few words from a seven-year-old to her mother's 'helper' Kathleen, who had just picked her up from school and they were walking on a path through a housing estate. They passed a patch of soil that had dandelions growing on it but they were almost finished, dead.

The child, Emma, remarked on this to Kathleen, and in her 'thoughtful' way, for a seven-year-old, she asked, 'How do they die, the flowers, and they come back next year, but when people die, how come they don't come back it would be nice...?'

'Beyond your physical self, beyond your thoughts and emotions, there lies a realm within you that is pure potential. From this place, anything and everything is possible. Even miracles. Especially miracles.

Deepak Chopra

CHAPTER FOUR

PEOPLE MAY NOT REMEMBER what you say or what you do but they will never forget how you made them feel.

Anne Davies has a twin brother Paul, but it was always Anne who was susceptible to the other side of life; Anne had 'seen things' from a very early age. They were from a close Catholic family, their parents, Len and Marjorie, were devoted to each other.

When their mother Marjorie, as well as having other health problems, developed Alzheimer's disease' (very badly), Len, her dad, was devastated, but devoted himself, never wavering, to her care. Len had health problems himself, including with the heart, but he looked after Marjorie for almost five years until he was admitted to hospital, dying there in October 2001, three days before their Diamond Wedding anniversary.

Anne's mother Marjorie was admitted to a care cottage hospital and it was there that the wondrous evidence of the closeness of the spirit world demonstrated in abundance, the love – in which we are all held.

After the funeral of her father Len, Anne visited the hospital as usual, and was surprised when her mother, who hardly ever communicated, quietly asked, 'Where's Len?' She asked again, 'Where is Len?' and just at the same time, a song came on the radio, 'There's a Place for US'. It was their favourite song.

Not long after, extra, extraordinary evidence took place, again at the hospital, and this time involving the nurse Sarah, who was busy attending to a patient in the cubicle opposite to the one Marjorie was in.

Suddenly, the sound of two happy voices, coming from the cubicle opposite (the one Marjorie was in), made her stand, motionless, breath held, in complete astonishment! How could this be? Top security in the hospital meant that only she herself would know of any potential visitor and be able to activate the security for only those given permission to be on the ward. No such request had been made.

Sarah, forgetting all else, listened, and listened, then quietly, nervously, crossed the ward to the cubicle opposite and peered through a gap in the curtain.

There sat a man and a woman (Marjorie), holding hands laughing, talking, with not a care in the world, completely engrossed in each other.

Now quite out of her depth as to whatever was happening, Sarah, more than puzzled by it all, but not worried, having seen the situation and the wonderful happiness of the two people involved, felt somehow not worried about it but full of happiness herself. Light-hearted and easy in her mind, she returned to the patient in the cubicle where she had been busy and could have laughed out loud at her position; here she was, in charge of a ward, not knowing and not having a clue and not even caring, as to what was going on.

Later that day Marjorie's daughter Anne visited as usual. She was stunned and incredulous as she listened to the tale of the visitor. Her mother was the same quiet, uninterested self, but on thinking about it, was there not a little sign of perhaps a more happy, contented demeanour about her... she wondered?

At the end of the visit, after leaving her mother, Anne and Sarah sat down to have a really in-depth talk about it. Although Sarah gave Anne a carefully worded description of the visitor – allowing for the fact that she was in a state of shock herself – the big question remained; how could he have got into the ward in the first place, then straight into the right cubicle? Who was he anyway? There was no doubt about the tight security and the sincerity of Sarah, while Anne was finding it difficult to focus her mind on it at all, including descriptions!

Then Paul arrived, Anne's twin brother. His amazement was as almost unbelieving as the others were, but after much discussion, everything pointed to one thing and one identity, Len. Len in his true love, his life's love, had broken through the barrier of death to rejoin Marjorie, to give her comfort and support, love enough to keep her content until they could be reunited; all love; forever love, the power of love, all the way.

*Len had been a service engineer in the navy. During the Second World War, he was in a Russian convoy when the ship was in serious trouble, the Captain saying to the crew – 'If you believe in God, get down on your knees and pray.' Len did, and vowed that if he survived, he would become a Catholic, which he did.

Anne's mother lived another three years after the experience (Len's visit).

Anne, who had stopped going to church some time previously, decided to go again, which she did, and has never looked back.

★

Going back a few years, when I talked to people at random and asked them their feelings about the other side of life, the so called 'paranormal' and did they believe, the ready answer was often, 'oh I don't believe in anything like that' (pause) – (big pause), then, 'but there was one thing.' There were so many 'one thing's in the answers that it began to feel as though there were very few who did not believe! Now, a few years later, I am positively convinced that although church attendance numbers are going down (which I have already mentioned in a previous chapter), there is a strengthening of belief, of a 'something' we can all call on in our time of need – and a great belief in angels.

An assistant in the bookshop I visited last week, hearing about my writing, was keen to tell me how finding the spiritual in his life had changed things for him so much that *that* was more unbelievable than anything! He would be in his thirties and seemingly continuing his studies but since the change came about for him, continuing with a new, happy, contented outlook so much so that he could honestly say he could 'get high on life'.

A lull in this otherwise usually busy shop, gave an older woman assistant time to listen to our conversation and she just had to join in with, 'Some years ago, I was in a launderette waiting for the end of the wash. It was very cold in there although there was a heater. I bent forward to turn it up but as I did so, *a strong hand pulled me back*. I have never forgotten that experience and know that it was a marker in my life to know someone cares.'

There is now such an explosion of belief (there always has been but in certain 'other times' a reluctance to tell), but now, with people keen to tell their stories, however dramatic, or seemingly unbelievable or perhaps trivial. Nothing is trivial if it is from Spirit. Nothing, if we are so privileged as to have a link, some connection with the other side.

Gary is a really nice regular guy, as is the expression sometimes still used. He has recently retired from teaching, a historian, and I rarely meet up with him for a chat although we are neighbours, but I have known him for years. We are, another expression I like to use, 'ships that pass in the night'.

Just over this last year, Gary had an experience that really threw him, knocked him sideways so to speak, right out of his usual, pleasant, routine/life style and he seemed pleased to meet up – accidentally of course – with me, and told me his story.

Gary had been to his cousin's funeral, a few days earlier, a cousin he had grown up with and they had always been good mates, but he could not get over the emotional grief, the terrible downer he had felt during the service, this overpowering depth of sadness leading to the thought 'What's it all about, anyway?

He remembered feeling overpowered by the three pieces of music played during the service, how he had reacted to them and knew he would never forget them, but to Gary, the most extraordinary thing of all was; back home, feeling drained, worn out, he tried to have a rest in the conservatory. He put the radio on and the music immediately played was the first piece played at the funeral. This was strange, to Gary, yes, very strange, and not helping his troubled, sad, feeling at all; the next day, again resting, he put the radio on and the music played was the second piece played at the funeral.

Later on, in the car, his wife turned on the car radio to hear a performance of the third piece of music, all three pieces played at the funeral, now really giving Gary food for thought.

★

Here is another instance of a guiding hand on the shoulder. Remember over a previous page, the woman in the launderette feeling the guiding hand on her shoulder, well here is another instance of the same, but this time on the shoulder of a three-year-old child, Alex.

Alex was the only witness to the horrific rape and murder of his mother, on Wimbledon Common. The date was Wednesday, 15th July 1992. You will probably remember this chilling tale, but now, just to give you a glimpse of the background:

Born into a loving home, Alex had parents, though not well off, determined to give him the best start in life. His father was out at work, leaving him and Rachel his mother to their own devises.

Rachel was a wonderful mother in every way, planning, as he grew, outings into the countryside, the parks, Wimbledon Common, all the while fostering in him a love of nature in all its forms. When he reached two, they bought him a puppy he named Molly. Molly, he chose from the brood. She grew with him, both relishing their exciting times together, seeing, and doing, playing. They soon became best friends.

One day, over the weekend, the four of them, Mother, Father, Alex and Molly returned home after yet another long walk in the country, to find a badly injured bird lying outside their front door. It had a broken wing. His father came back from the house with a box to carry it in and tried to make it as comfortable as possible, then the two of them scratched around in the back garden for worms and insects and other treats to feed it using tweezers. Alex had given it the name 'Birdie'.

The next morning he woke up to a loud burst of birdsong; he was so happy to see the little bird looking happy and content which kept up for a few days, then, one afternoon he found him lying on the bottom of the box, stiff and cold. Upset and worried, he called to his mother, 'What has happened to Birdie?' He does not need his body any more, she tried to explain to him; the part that is really him has gone somewhere else now.

A few days later, his mother took him to the local library, the children's section, where she picked out certain books that were dealing with the subject of death. They took the books home and read them together while she tried to explain that perhaps I would be sad that Birdie had gone, but he was now free and his broken wing was not hurting him any longer. He had gone to a beautiful place, where he could be happy. 'We are not our bodies,' she explained. 'The body is only like clothes we put on for a little while.'

Deeply upset, it was only days before when Alex had been watching a video cartoon about a baby dinosaur that 'had been separated' from his mother by an earthquake. Heartbroken, the baby dinosaur searched and searched for her, and when he did finally find her, she was so weak and frail she finally collapsed to the ground, dying. 'Please get up, get up,' he cried but she could not. She told him to carry on to the Great Valley and promised to be with him always, even if he couldn't see her.

It was not long after, they were walking on Wimbledon Common as usual, Alex, his mother and Molly. Passing the little grave they had made for Birdie, they didn't stop, Alex more quiet in his mind now, remembering his mother's soothing words as she explained to him about death.

Walking on, Molly at their side, they made their way to the pond, then headed back up the hill again. Uphill and down dale by a small stream then down another path, where it was darker, and then, as if sensing something was wrong, they both turned their heads to the right. A man suddenly appeared out of nowhere – he had a bag over his shoulder and lurching towards Alex he grabbed him roughly and threw him onto the muddy ground, his face forced into the mud.

'Seconds later, my mother collapsed next to me. There were no screams. Everything was silent.' He looked down at his mother lying on the ground beside him. She looked peaceful.

'"Get up, Mummy, get up," I said louder. "Get up, Mummy," I shouted with all my strength.'

'She was gone. Just like Birdie, she had disappeared. I was very young, and yet, at that moment, on some deep level, I knew she was never coming back. My heart was completely broken.

'Around me was absolute silence. The woodland was peaceful – even though my mother's body lay beside me on the ground. Even though my face was swollen and bruised and my clothes splattered with blood. I began running out of the woods, not sure where I was going. I was flooded with pain, but felt *a guiding hand on my shoulder* ushering me gently out of the trees.'

Alex tells us how strangers ran towards him, seeing his 'battered face and blood-splattered clothes' did everything they could to help him; 'They were very kind.'

Now twenty-six, he had returned to London often enough over the years, visiting close family and friends but this visit would be different. He wanted to return, and for the first time, visit Wimbledon Common and the scene of his mother's murder. He had never before felt the need or even the slightest desire to return there, but for some reason, the time had now come.

Without too much difficulty, as if belying all the years that had passed between, he found his way back. His thoughts tumbled here there and everywhere as he moved nearer to the scene; it felt like only yesterday when life was so sweet, with not a care in the world. In seconds he became the only witness to the brutal attack and murder that changed everything. Where had the time gone? The travelling, the move to live in France, mainly to avoid the press and all the hounding he and his dad had gone through then, once again, a quick 'fly by night' move to Spain.... As he reached the edge of the common and the surroundings became familiar, yes, it was all as yesterday and now he had this overwhelming feeling of 'going home'.

He walked along the path he had walked along only minutes after the attack, and felt his mother's presence 'all around me', stronger than ever before. Reaching the spot where it had happened, he knelt down on the soft, damp earth, hands clasped tightly together in prayer, and gave thanks; thanks for his life and for his understanding; his blessings and the knowledge of being looked after, guided; thanks for his wonderful mother and everything she gave him. 'I will always love you.' Thanks, thanks, thanks; heartfelt and heartful. For making all the pieces of the puzzle come together, knowing all was well and how it had to be.

'Molly, Molly, Molly,' brought him suddenly back to the moment, 'Molly, Molly,' a man calling his dog. 'I was certain. A higher power was watching over me, making sure that everything was perfect, telling me, letting me know by sending a sign.'

The light now beginning to fade, Alex made his way back to the station, fuller, richer, and yes, certain.

It seems to be that as we become aware of the help and guidance available to us from the Spirit World, so we will see it in uncountable ways. Signs and symbols; coincidences – remember the words 'a coincidence is God's way of working a miracle anonymously; evidence found in that 'unexpected phone call' that changed everything. A meeting 'out of the blue' heralding in changes wanted, but believed to be impossible, suddenly happening. An accident that turned out to be a precursor of good tidings! A misunderstanding – that led to all sorts of complications, leading to 'well how did all that come about?' and very grateful that it did.

Once the amazing evidence of help and the love shown to us from the 'other side' of life becomes a reality in our way of thinking, **it does change everything.** We know that whatever happens, we do not walk alone; remembering, as the woman in the launderette discovered when she believed she was 'saved' by an invisible hand pulling her back – accepting it as a marker in her life 'to know someone cares'.

It has been proved that as human beings we already have that natural, deep, ingrained sense of a higher side to our being than the merely physical. We are first and foremost 'spirit', in a physical body that we need to inhabit our earth plane.

Sir Alister Hardy, FRS was a brilliant scientist who made his name as a brilliant marine biologist. He spent several years at sea on the *Discovery* as Chief Zoologist on a prolonged Arctic expedition. He was a naturalist, a man interested in all forms of nature, life, the Universe, writing many books, giving lectures and he ran an exceptionally successful department as a professor of zoology, at Oxford. Sir Alister was the founder of the Religious Experience Research Centre, now situated at the University of Wales.

Being aware of the Spirit world since childhood, he tells us, 'I have had, during my childhood, several experiences where I felt very strongly that a power in which I could be wholly confident was acting for and around me.'

He continues, telling us of 'his marvellous experience' as he was walking along Marylebone Road one day. He was 'suddenly seized with an extraordinary sense of great joy and exultation' as though a 'marvellous beam of spiritual power' had shot through him, linking him in a rapture with the world, the Universe, Life with a capital L, and all beings around him.

Gradually, over the years, he was drawn to the thought of the countless experiences from people there must be out there, just waiting to be heard; to be kept, to be recorded, for others to share. It was Sir Alister Hardy we have to thank, for the founding of The Religious Experience Research Centre, now known as RERC, coming to fruition, finally settling at the University of Wales, in the year 2000.

The first chapter in Sir Alister's book, *The Spiritual Nature of Man*, from which the earlier extracts were taken, has the heading, 'Spiritual Feeling In A Scientific Age'.* (Those few words as the heading, say so much, cover so much and have such a depth of meaning for each one of us in this strange new world we find ourselves part of.)

In the book, he tells us, 'Over the years, my colleagues and I have collected together over four thousand first-hand accounts which show that a large number of people even today possess a deep awareness of a benevolent non-physical power, wholly beyond, and far greater than, the individual self.'

It was about 2oo3 when I made my way to the University of

Wales (three trains), and it seems that I was the first researcher to darken its doors. I 'was met' with great friendliness and interest in my work – starting my second book, which was to be focused on the 'so called paranormal', and encouraged to make full use of all facilities. Even in that early stage of the department, there were plenty.

Help was always at hand as I sorted through letters and documents and any information pertaining to the – what I like to call 'the other side of life'. Much time was involved in the four or five days I was there, writing out, by hand, many of the fascinating experiences held in this amazing archive. It was good; all of it, and now time to leave.

Setting off for home, happy and delighted with myself for the amount of work I had accomplished, and the lovely people I had met, I faced my 'three trains' in a different, more relaxed state of mind to my journey down. (Little did I know of the experiences to come.)

The station was quiet and as I sat on one of the benches waiting for the first of my trains to arrive, I had an unexpected surprise. The slow, almost majestic entrance on the other side of the track, of a smart-looking train with words – (emblazoned in gold all along its side) stretching on and on as it continued its slow pace through the station – by Dillon Thomas; My favourite poet.

Well how about that? I thought, taking in every word, thrilled to bits at what I had seen. What an excellent send-off after my special week.

★

The pattern of travel was to be a long train journey, then a short one connecting me up to the third and final long journey from York to home, Newcastle on Tyne.

On this, the first of my long train journeys, I sat opposite a woman called Margaret, and we soon found ourselves having a laugh about 'nothing' I suppose, but it was good to 'be settled' and we both appreciated having each other to talk to. The talk remained light-hearted for a good part of the journey, and then, a sudden change. I had explained that I was visiting Lampeter to do some work at the university, but simply kept it as general studies and Margaret did not question anything anyway.

I cannot remember how the conversation changed but then I heard a most heart-breaking story that Margaret had suffered, which she had overcome, but for some reason wanted to confide in me. As she told her story, I gradually intervened with my belief; my experiences, the other side of life, and what I was really researching at the university. She was fascinated then added words that I will never forget and which I have used sometimes in my writing.

Margaret had carried such a weight of sorrow and for a long time, so lost and alone, she had decided to take her own life. She just could not seem to reach anyone, no one cared; yes, people would have a laugh and share tales but no one made any move to befriend her…probably they did not see her need, and she had not confided in anyone. This situation continued indefinitely. She believed there was nothing left for her, so why carry on?

She was so lonely, depressed and unsettled in her mind, she kept trying to plan a date to take her own life, then changing it. Another date was changed. Another date changed. The final one she planned had a determination about it lacking in the other attempts and somehow she knew – 'This had to be it.'

Margaret had 'made her peace', nothing to stop her now, and then suddenly, from nowhere it seemed, there was a knock on the door, followed by a ring of the bell.

A knock on the door, a ring of the bell that said to Margaret that someone cared, and they did care, as she later found out.

While telling me the tale, even though it was a long time ago, I can still see her face alight with happiness at the remembrance of it all.

Laughing, we repeated the magical words together a few times, words of hope, joy, and best of all, caring.

The knock on the door, a ring of the bell that says someone cares.

★

York station was packed and so was the train. With Its corridors bulging, it seemed like everybody was on this train. Reluctantly I joined the throng but carrying lightweight luggage it was not too bad. Then I met my astonishing windfall!

I could see, coming up ahead, the wide area between coaches, filled with young lads from the army, possibly new recruits. There were six or seven of them and, as I made to pass, one of them caught me gently by the arm and said, 'Come and sit with us, you won't find a seat along there, look, a good seat here on a kit bag,' and then he made it two. Not really sure, however, I joined them, and was soon made to feel welcome and comfortable perched up on the two kit bags.

The young soldiers were about eighteen, fit, well and full of fun. They had been on a special course partly, I believe, to see if they really did want to join up, which they did. Staying at barracks down South, near London, these Geordie lads were full of talk about the difficult, challenging things they had had to go through but were seemingly pleased with their assessments and still sure the army was the life for them.

A tall, blonde-haired lad seemed to be their leader; he was the one who took my arm and insisted I sit with them and made sure I was comfortable. He was also the one who, only once or twice, had to call out, 'Language, lads, remember, language!'

They were all very excited to be going home (Geordie-Land), and after a most successful course which they had revelled in, and which had probably sealed their future in the army. What could be better...but there was one thing they were all excited about and I could tell that they wanted to share it with me, but were rather apprehensive.

Their leader on the course, the main officer who was responsible for them, they all agreed was brilliant. They could not praise him enough. They talked about his 'interest in them, and his consideration, and how carefully he explained things'. All I could do was 'add' a word or two here and there – good, excellent, and so on. Continuing their spiel, finally, with, 'We could tell you something, but you wouldn't believe it.. Anyway, it was not quite 'finally', because finally, they did end this part of the conversation with, 'He is a healer.'

Trying hard to assure me that it was true, they had seen it for themselves, apparently one of their team had, on the first morning there, fallen over and hurt his foot – and as a result would probably have had to sit out on exercises on the field, gym, everywhere. This was when they discovered their officer was a healer. He explained as much as he thought necessary to them while they watched him treat the patient. Probably prayers included – I am not sure about all the details, they told me so much, but they witnessed swelling disappearing, a gradual strengthening of the injured foot, and within a day or so their soldier friend was once more in action, and on the team.

★

The journey rattled on with that familiar rhythmic throbbing of wheels on track while the lads continued telling me – taking turns to speak and listening carefully to each other – about their course, always ending up with some little anecdote about Mick, their officer.

Soon, I was to find out that Mick, was not only a healer, but he had explained to them that he was also a medium. Waiting for my certain questioning of 'what is a medium?' but as I said nothing, it was quickly brushed over with examples of evidence.

Mick had given evidence of a Spirit World their grandparents and other loved ones had gone to and evidential happenings in their lives that no one outside their families could have known.

So enthralled by it all were these young lads, they would never, they *could* never, forget Mick, their officer in charge, healer and medium and the wisdom he tried to instil in them as a safeguard for their future happiness and success.

Reflecting on it all later, at home, I felt a big smile beaming not only on my face, but all through me. Never could I forget those lovely lads and Mick, their healer, medium, officer in charge; then there was Margaret and the all-important lesson on caring; the ring of the bell, the knock on the door. The smart **L O N G** train with words by Dillon Thomas, my favourite poet, proudly emblazoned all along it.

What a journey, what a week! Strange to think that I had visited the university to read and record the experiences of other people, and on the way home, had three of my own.

★

Experiences; is it not true to say that most of us, if not all, have had at some time in our lives that special 'something' we know was 'real', even though we maybe could not quite understand at the time. Now however, could it be partly due to the amazing technology we are living in and with, that there are not so many 'disbelievers' in the other side of life, the Spirit World, even though church attendance numbers are apparently dropping. It could be, as in America, people are finding their own way to acknowledge a belief in another side of life as the opportunity to do so arises. Groups are meeting in local community centres and the number varies from perhaps half a dozen to at least sixty, meeting every two weeks as in one centre I know about, and growing with each meeting.

We enjoy listening to the experiences of others and telling

our own, and in the process we might have such a good feeling of – is it 'belonging'? An inner sense, an emotion that we know is real encompassing us in a strong bond of comfort. This is what is 'known' as (even in a tiny whisper of a thought), contact with the other side of life, the spirit world.

Science and medicine are now moving closer to the reality of a spirit world, as forecast it would happen by the ancients. By the mediums, philosophers, historians, and as we witnessed in our 'now' time, not so long ago, with the headline news, the first recognition *of the movement of artificial limbs,* through the discovery – the amazing truth of 'the power of thought'…real, true, and including you and me… all of us, have the power of thought.

There are countless ways of making contact with the other side of life and the danger of trying is minimal as long as we have sincerity of purpose, love in our hearts, care and attention to the presentation of our attempt and NEVER, never ever, treating it as a game.

The power of prayer is essential in our efforts; remember our serious intention is to reach over into another dimension and although we may have it in our hearts and minds that it is a trillion miles away…really, it is only a thought. A thought, is a prayer.

Fortune telling, which has been around for centuries, probably since the beginning, continues to be popular and it could be a reading with a gypsy, a telling in palmistry, a ribbon reading, used for thousands of years, a reading of the tea-leaves, numerology, telepathy, meditation, to name only a few. In other words, to quote;

'There is a belief in what transcends the "every day".'

America recently gave notice that one of their biggest sources of income is from Mind Body and Spirit Shops; with facilities for readings, healing, and there are many and varied methods of healing; shelves devoted to scores of books relating to the subject (the other side of life), magazines, newspapers and of course Spiritualist Churches.

As well as visiting a medium or attending a Spiritualist Church or perhaps being part of 'a private development class', one of the best known methods of communication is probably through the Weejie Board, with the correct spelling, 'OUIJA BOARD. While most people seem to know of its dangers, if practised honestly and sincerely with the highest and best of intentions, it can be superb as I will try to prove to you at the start of the next chapter, chapter five, which has the title 'OUIJA BOARD: NO-YES-PERHAPS' …

We ignore the spiritual as sleepers numb to reality in their pursuit of dreams.

CHAPTER FIVE

Nothing is certain and everything is possible.

OUIJA BOARD : NO-YES-PERHAPS! (pronounced Weejie Board).

WE MET HARRY, MY husband Peter and I when he moved into a bungalow on the plantation where we lived, in Rand Berg, near Johannesburg, South Africa.

Alice, the owner of the plantation, a very kindly, caring person, asked us to look after Harry as he struggled to come to terms with the loss of his wife Janet, a few months previously. He missed her badly, she was his rock, and he felt he had taken her for granted, and desperately wished he had shown her more love and appreciation over the years. Harry was a successful business-man travelling widely, and had now bought a sugar plantation near Jo'burg, but out in the wilds.

He was truly in a bad way, and Alice, knowing our interest in spiritualism, believed we were the ones to help him. He had talked to her about his grief and questioned, 'Was there really such a thing as life after death?'

We were pleased to be able to spend time with him and do our best to assure him that yes, there was, but for some reason, he never did get to join us at a Spiritualist meeting or church on a Sunday evening.

The weeks went by and Harry moved into a hotel in Johannesburg prior to his moving out to his plantation. We kept in touch but I wished and prayed that we could do more to help him. He had asked me to name a medium he could visit in London, apparently money was no objection, but I was reluctant to take that step. Then I had an idea. Why not arrange a night with a couple of good friends and Harry, and have a session with the Ouija Board? It would be an interesting, hopefully, happy send-off for him. My husband was dead set against it. 'No, No, No.' But I insisted … (he knew the old story when I had had a troubled sad night along with friends, in England, probably because of a badly managed session with it). I insisted that this would be different. We were doing it out of love, sincerity, trying our best to help someone going off on his own to a new life, a broken man we *had* to help, and this was the best way I felt that we could.

We played suitable music in our home all week. There were lovely flowers, prayers said as usual but on this week more than ever, anything I could think of to have the right atmosphere in preparation for the big night to come; and come it did. Two friends joined us and we were all set, a special supper waiting for us at the end of a wonderful evening, but no Harry.

Communication was not easy then in South Africa, I had to go out to a centre on the plantation to try to contact him at his hotel, as he was leaving in a matter of days. He was worried about us and not getting to our evening, but an old friend had arrived unexpectedly to see him before he left Johannesburg.

Deeply disappointed, and feeling a little shamefaced, I had made such a fuss about this whole carry-on, and now what? – however, we had the session, prayers and all, as planned.

True to form, the glass moved and pushed and scraped around the board as if its very life depended on it. On and on, with no sense at all, as if it was in a race it sped from one letter to another until it finally settled on the simple word 'cat'. 'Cat!' and that was it. After a break for supper, we returned to find the same theme, cat, cat, cat, never ending.

Allowing plenty of time to get to the church later, we called at the hotel to say our goodbyes to Harry who was in a very sombre mood, and not like anyone about to embark on a new, exciting life, as he was. Apologising again for his absence, we reassured him that it was just as well he wasn't there. 'Just a waste of time, Harry, better you stayed with your friend,' and so on as we tried to change the subject. He obviously wanted to know just what had happened, referring back to it every now and again... 'But what did it say?' etc. etc. 'Nothing, Harry, nothing!" we insisted, then finally, we had to explain it all to him, the glass whizzing around every letter of the alphabet, jumping around, no sense to it at all, pointing out, in disgust, that there was only one word spelt out, over and over again, dozens of times... 'Cat.'

I can hardly remember what happened next. Harry, who had been sitting on the edge of his bed (we were in the armchairs), let out such a shout, with tears, sobs, cries unimaginable from such a steady, sensible, grown-up man, that I flew over to comfort him, cradling him in my arms, but at this point there seemed to be no healing.

Finally, through the sobs and what appeared to be signs of joy – we got the message. Janet, his wife, was a successful 'bowler', winning trophies from all over the country, and proud to be the Captain of a South African team for Ladies. Members of the team had a special name written on the bottom of their bowls. The name written on Janet's was 'Cat'.

★

Since the beginning, the beginning of time, the beginning of everything, all sorts of phenomena has been in evidence, with early man and animals and all creatures looking to nature for answers as to their survival, their everyday existence, seeking to understand changes in the weather, the position of the sun, the moon, the changing seasons. Early man would chant in praise to the elements what we now call prayers, giving thanks 'for all good things' while seeking for advice with regard to 'moving on', a celebration of a birth or marriage or getting through a particularly rough patch.

Over time, however, and by time I mean a few thousand years and more, while things changed, the need for the 'special ones', those who seemed to be able to tap into that 'unexplainable something' later called (and we still call) 'God', was there, and as important and *is* as important, as it ever has been.

This is proved every day in our now highly charged technical age, where, although the numbers are steadily dropping in attendance at churches, people are finding their own way to link in, to find that help and comfort we all crave from time to time as we pass through life.

From the earliest man, there were those who looked among themselves for the ones who had proved themselves to be healers, prophets, mediums, and suitable leaders – these traits were also around in the animal kingdom; never underestimate the wisdom of 'all creatures great and small'.

*It is sad to think of the suffering such chosen ones had to endure, remembering the tragedy of Joan of Arc and the countless men and women who fell because of their calling and determination to help others, evidenced throughout the centuries; suffering horrendous tortures, vilification and then for them, if they were lucky, merciful death. Helping and caring and then to be branded as evil, the devil's own, evil witches...innocent, cursed and hounded out of villages with nowhere to go and nobody to care but we can read about one witch, who miraculously did not end in such dire circumstances. She was known as Mother Shipton, the Yorkshire witch.

Mother Shipton was born in a cave (now one of the oldest tourist attractions in England), at Knaresborogh, in Yorkshire. She was born in 1488 of poor parentage and when they died, and left her destitute, she somehow continued to live in the old house looking to the parish for help, of which apparently there was none.

(I am reminded of an old expression, to be 'hard up and parish dammed'.)

Known as the Yorkshire witch, she was also known as an English Soothsayer and prophetess with the first publication of her prophecies in 1641, eighty years after her reported death. Her prophecies, written on scrolls, were discovered a long time after her death.

She has the name Agatha Shipton in many of the old documents written about her. Although there are discrepancies in some of the documents, it seems to be a proven fact that she did exist and was an excellent prophetess, not only foretelling important events at the time but major changes in the world, which we can now verify.

It is written that all who saw her and heard her held her in great esteem, shown in the writing on a stone erected to her memory near Clifton, a mile from the city of York – the whole area a well-known tourist spot such is the continued interest she inspires.

The EpItaph on the stone reads:

Here lies she who never lied,
Whose skill often has been tried
Her prophecies shall still survive
And ever keep her name alive.

The introduction to her story, according to some of the scripts of the time, sounds like the start of a good fairy story, one that, in any age or time, we would all enjoy reading:

'In the reign of Henry VII lived a woman called Agatha Shipton at Knaresborogh in Yorkshire. Her parents were poor and left her destitute. She had no-one and had to ask for help from the parish (but better to beg?).

(Hard up and parish dammed.)

She did get by, manage, as we might say now, with neighbours and others taking a big interest in her as she obviously had something about her that was different and in time, her very words were often found to be worth repeating.

Her future prophecies linked in with the already great belief in Tudor England in such things. There was a great belief, in every level of Tudor England, in every level of Tudor Society, reaching a climax during the dangerous times of Tudor England in the 1530s with Queens and courtiers beheaded, monasteries destroyed and rebels hanged from trees. And so, as her prophecies, predictions, came to pass, so spreading her name far and wide, we can only wonder, marvel, to think that all this could happen *then; in the* fifteenth century, without the internet.

Her words began to be esteemed as oracles – predictions that Henry VIII would win the war in France and described how it would come about with an accuracy that in itself was astonishing to behold.

Her prophesies rang true to include the Great Death in London verified by the Great Plague in 1665 (the greatest that had been known in these latter centuries) – 'and many houses laid low'; 'the great conflagration of fire (1666)'.

In a vision she saw the accession of Lady Jane Grey and the execution; the execution of Mary Queen of Scots and the defeat of the Spanish Armada. Other prophesies from Mother Shipton concern future times, put in rhyme,

'for in those wondrous days far off the women shall adapt a craze.

To dress like men and trousers wear, and cut off all
their locks of hair.
They'll ride astride with brazen brow
as witches do on broomsticks now.

In another rhyme 'a carriage without horse will go, disaster
fill the world with woe.'

These are only a few of the many modern events she foretold.

The prophesies of Mother Shipton were linked in with Tudor
England, where there was a great belief in such things at every
level of society. She saw Wolsey's fate and the dangerous times of
Tudor England with Queens and courtiers beheaded, monasteries
destroyed, rebels hanged from trees.

But in spite of all the dangers and jealousies and mishaps she
must have endured and survived, she lived to a great age, living to
earn the honourable epitaph – and from her fellow countrymen,
copied from the writing on the old stone erected to her memory,
the last lines of which are:

'Her prophecies shall still survive
And ever keep her name alive.'
Mother Shipton, the Yorkshire Witch

We all know that we don't have to be a witch or a wizard
or even a psychic to have a paranormal experience. Things are
happening, messages for us from the other side of life, perhaps in
our ordinary, everyday lives that can make us sit up and take notice
and there are also many ordinary experiences that we register,
maybe wonder about for a while, then shrug our shoulders and
forget. It is not easy to communicate between the two worlds and
we should be very grateful for any message that we may receive,
even if it takes a while to understand and work out.

Once we do understand and see the truth and care for us that is with it, there follows the amazement, the sheer joy, the uplift, to think that such a thing is really possible.

CHAPTER SIX

(THIS is a story within a story)
TO TELL It as It WAS

Southampton Airport

JULY 2014

HAVING SPENT A FEW hours in a comfortable little cafe upstairs, writing, now was about time to move into the main waiting area for flight departures and where I had a pleasant conversation with an Irish woman sitting a few seats away. We were sitting on the front row of a long line of chairs, not many people around, and her husband sitting, again, a few seats away from her. I suppose you could say we were spreading out. It was a very long line – of chairs.

The couple were from Dublin, Margaret and Reggie, and immediately reminded me of Marty and Alice, my close friends when I lived in London, who were also from Dublin. Marty and Alice and I had gone through a cocktail of life's experiences together over the years, good and not so good, but a nicer and more genuine couple you could not meet...now long passed away into the spirit world.

The conversation with Margaret turned to my writing and while she seemed to be particularly interested, Reggie was absorbed in working on his laptop and papers. The time flew by as Margaret and I chatted away together, about forty minutes, and I wish we had swopped names and addresses. Their flight was called and Margaret carefully collected her belongings, reminding Reggie that he had the small case as well as his coat and laptop, then made her way to the departure gate waving to me with a big smile as if to say, 'Nice to have met you.' I wish we had swopped names and addresses!

What I am about to tell you is no exaggeration, no 'imagination', but 'what' and 'how' it happened. (Oh how I wish I had taken their name and address!)

Reggie collected his belongings, Margaret still calling to him to hurry up but instead, on standing up, he turned towards me, one leg ready to come over to see me and the other ready to step back towards Margaret and the exit – making a sort of little dance, arms and head forward, struggling with his luggage and his voice, well...

He must have been listening to *some* of our conversation, as I tried to give Margaret a flimsy idea of a chapter for my new book, but...! He didn't seem to be interested or *really* interested, anyway, he could not have gleaned anything from our short, scrappy conversation.

In writing this, I have re-lived that afternoon at the airport many times and can still see, vividly, the animation, the determination, in Reggie's movements towards me, as if on a mission. His voice, his face, as he called out something like 'Shellek' again and again; still I didn't pick up what he was saying, and then he called something like – 'You must do it,' me moving yet closer and Margaret still calling out to him, agitated herself by now, but still he continued, 'You must do it, write it down.' Having heard him call the name out a few times now, I began to place it as 'Shackleton', a famous explorer, me calling back, 'Yes,' and showing him pen and paper... still not sure of what he was trying to tell me, I am mainly aware of hearing the echoing of

'You must do it …don't forget,' laptop and case flying along with him as he finally joined Margaret – then quiet – all quiet – they were gone. I was stunned. What was all that about?

I have already mentioned Marty and Alice and how close we were and through music too. We were three musicians working and sometimes performing together. – 'Close are the ties that bind' – but this, well, this was something else. They were both interested in all my work and would always try hard to help me whenever they could and now, what was the link between Reggie and something to do with Shackleton? Maybe it was a great opportunity… 'a great story'; now I was really beginning to wonder – could this be a way of Marty and Alice getting a message through to me – and Jean, the same?

Jean, another close London friend (I was very lucky), had tried for years to get through to me the significance of the same story, 'Shackleton'. Jean was a great reader and scholar (I have just a faint memory of her talking to me about it). Obviously wanting me to study it and she even bought me a poetry book by T. S. Eliot whose famous poem, 'The Waste Land', featured a most wonderful part of the Shackleton story, of which I WAS OBLIVIOUS; and a tape recording of his poem, 'The Waste Land' – Shackleton, the, 'special' one, *is* this what this is all about?

Now we are spot on the message, the reason for this strange incident, which I will try to explain as we travel on through the story but for the moment, can we return to the start of this wonderful adventure; August 8th 1914? We can come to the main point I am trying to make later. (Much later.)

★

August 8th 1914, and a crew of twenty-seven, with their leader, Sir Ernest Shackleton, set sail from Plymouth in the *Endurance* for the Antarctic.

Sir Ernest Shackleton was one of the most renowned

polar explorers of his day. Having already been on two Arctic expeditions, and now intent on yet another Arctic mission, he and his crew were travelling to the south, deep in the frozen waters of Antartica to claim one of the last prizes in exploration, the First crossing, *on foot*, of the Antarctic continent.

There was a strain of bad feeling among some of the public about this expedition. As Shackleton was trying to drum up support (and money), to help with the massive expense of such an undertaking, the people were understandably focused and worried about the war and questioning why the expedition was about to start out now – surely the men and all involved should have been enlisting as a force in the war?

He, Shackleton, had already sent a cable to First Lord of the Admiralty Churchill and the government offering their services in the war along with their ship and all the equipment. He received a grateful telegram back from Churchill in reply thanking them all but that they were 'to proceed as planned and concentrate on more glory for England'. Shackleton was relieved.

Early on in his career, he was known as a leader who put his men first. He was a great leader whom the men knew they could trust in any situation. Much because he was sincere, and he had gone through dreadful experiences in his two earlier expeditions, learning first and foremost to heed to the care of his men; throughout the whole of every trauma, every life-threatening experience that was to come – and there were plenty, he held and acted on that belief. Yes, he stopped a potential rebellion. He had major, unpopular decisions to make and put into action, which he did, but it was the innate goodness of the man that ever shone through.

It is well recorded that without any doubt about it, the men loved him.

One of the tales they liked to tell was, after a particularly bad night of storms and gales, he took breakfast around for each one of them as they awoke the following morning.

Shackleton had planned a short stay on South Georgia but was advised, because of the uncertainty of the weather, to stay longer and the short stay turned into a full month. This, however, did good in more ways than one, the men getting to know each other and becoming more familiar with their duties; supplies and cargo were replenished fully after the month. The men were rested and eager for the next stage of their journey, the *Endurance* steamed out of the Bay, heading South by Southeast. As early as the next day they passed numerous icebergs and blocked pack ice.

Days of thick mist opened onto clear days of brilliant sunshine but by now the game, with the *Endurance* stuck solid in ice flows, was avoiding the pack ice.

At times, they were able to gradually move the ship ahead, but then she was contained again by pack ice; then a gale that had blown continued all night blowing the ship further away from the direction of land – mist – ice – and more ice holding fast (and mercilessly to the frame of the ship).

IT **HAD** to happen. At five p.m, Shackleton gave the order to abandon ship. With heavy hearts and deep sadness the crew set about unloading as much as possible. They were 350 miles from the nearest land with days of loading, and dragging the lifeboats to be 'moved' to safety. As many supplies and equipment as possible were to be saved; here was a major life-saving operation to be got through, while all the time the men were numb with fatigue and the suddenness with which the end had come. Apparently, none of the diaries – each crew member had to keep a daily diary – show much concern for personal safety, but they pour forth their great sadness and heartbreak for the death of the ship. From her first entrance into the pack ice they had cheered her fighting spirit, 'noble', 'gallant', 'brave', 'our stout little ship', the words they had used with which to characterize her. Shackleton, in his writing said that he could not find words to write how he felt.

Of course it felt like the end of everything, and for Shackleton it was…but things change, and fate, as they call it, has a habit of stepping in and – you know the rest, we all face it at some time or other in our lives.

The next months passed, forever struggling, moving, making camp on treacherous ice floes, more moving, always hoping for something better, which wasn't there. It was hell on earth for the men, and we can only wonder in amazement and admiration, that this, what they were doing, was, as quoted, 'the impossible', Admire them, all the way. They did finally succeed, 'make it', as the expression goes, but that is for the end of the story and there is still a very long way to go, most of it not even touched on, in this account.

Illness, tempers frayed, nothing but ice, ice, and more ice; sleeping in wet bags, always freezing; food, they had to preserve as much as possible, scarce. Travelling for ten hours and moving only one mile. Some were thought to be going insane, having the first drink and hot food for three and a half days everything all around them relentless, unforgiving, threatening, countless weeks in open boats then they were at the beginning of an Antarctic winter as, finally, they arrived on Elephant Island.

> 'After meals of Seal Stakes, the men laid their bags on the solid earth and turned in for the night but didn't sleep much. It was hard for them to realise that they were on good old solid earth again and got up "too happy" to sleep but wandered around by the fire, ate and drank a little, have a smoke and talk over some of the past adventures.'

They soon discovered that although they had arrived on an abnormally fine day yet a grimmer, more hostile piece of land would be difficult to visualise. The morning after, a group of the crew set out in one of the boats to scout the coast for a better camp, returning in the evening with good news of a place seven miles down the coast. Early, next morning they were up and loading the boats again as best as they could...we can't really even imagine how dreadful and low they must have felt but they did it, in a fashion, leaving supplies stacked up in a safe place against rocks, maybe good to know they were there in case of an emergency! (However they soon found that food was abundant.)

Shackleton, noting the sickness among the men and that general behaviour was 'not satisfactory', he made his big announcement. A small party of men, under his command, would set out in the *James Caird* and make for the whaling stations of South Georgia. He explained carefully the sudden reason was that he knew help 'was needed' for the party remaining and as soon as possible. The island of South Georgia was 800 miles away and they would be travelling in an open boat to cross the most formidable ocean on the planet – in the winter. They all knew the horrors of the journey – but what else could be done?

The next busy days saw preparations made for both the men to be left behind and the crew leaving. As he planned and supervised decisions, Shackleton was meticulous in his overall judgement of both situations and crew. Each side was only too well aware of the seriousness of the situation and that it would take a lot of Luck???, Good Luck??? Good fortune??? And prayers for them, once parted, ever to meet again.

Suppressed tears, and a deep feeling of anguish must have been felt in both camps as the small boat made its way out into the waiting, lonely sea, the men left behind struggling to bid a cheery farewell to their ship mates of some months now, a long time, especially in their circumstances.

The *James Caird* was a small, open boat strong, sturdy, but with very cramped conditions, with only one small stove for cooking and making the hot drinks, every four hours, as Shackleton insisted on for the crew. Drinks for sustenance and well-being, to face the treacherous Antarctic winter weather with its pounding rain, sleet and snow and a fully fledged hurricane whipping off already mountainous seas, with the foam obscuring every trace of land.

They made it, Shackleton and his men, unbelievable as it was. They made the journey over the roughest, wildest tossing sea imaginable, in this small, open lifeboat named (and now forever famous) the *James Caird*. (Land ahoy – my words.)

As soon as possible, having secured the boat and their belongings on dry land, they prepared to face a formidable trek over unknown, treacherous territory with every day vital in seeking help for their comrades left behind.

They had no way of knowing which way to travel in this wasteland of white, no markers, no definable skyline or rock formations, nothing, nothing at all to give them even a little guidance as to where they were heading.

One day, stopping for a rest and something to eat, a small campfire they made seemed to give them not only a little brightness, but a feeling of uplift, of hope.

Then they noticed something about their leader, Shackleton. Was he more confident, were they all feeling more confident, or was it the way he moved, with assurance, like a man who knows exactly where he is going?

Time, months, did pass quickly, even for those on what they thought was a slow march, but they did have some 'help' and laughs on the way as they accidently slid down a steep mountainous slope to find themselves quicker than expected on what seemed to be – and proved to be – the right track, in their way of reckoning.

Further on, they started to see signs of life and then, on one bright morning, the distant outline of a whaling station.

Exhausted, weary, with no emotion visible at all on these unrecognisable faces and bodies, kindly sailors guided them into an office that Shackleton had been welcomed into many a time before.

Their bearded faces were black with blubber smoke, and their matted hair clotted with salt, hung almost to their shoulders. Their filthy clothes were in tatters. The few in the office who knew Shackleton were too shocked to speak while a Norwegian whaler who knew Shackleton well simply said, 'Me, I turn away and weep.'

They were looked after with much care and then it was all speed to arrange a rescue ship for the men left behind. Rescue was not as quick or as easy as Shackleton had expected and there was not a chance of an English ship, difficulties because of the war...? They did finally have the chance of other ships, but they were also unsuitable for such a dangerous journey with extreme bad weather and ice flows. After more weeks of waiting and disappointment and the worry Shackleton suffered over the men marooned on Elephant Island, they finally set sail in a small, steel-built tug steamer loaned to them by the Chilean government and with a Chilean crew...

Thinking deeply and quietly over the past weeks and months, Shackleton had to admit to having no doubt that Providence guided them, not only across those snowfields, but across the storm-white sea.

> 'I know that during that long, and racking march of thirty-six hours, over the mountains and glaciers of South Georgia, it seemed to me often that we were four, not three...The other two confessed to having the same feeling, that there was another person with us, as they had felt at the camp-fire, earlier on, when we were suddenly filled with confidence.'

It appears to be that Shackleton thought, what a wonderful, thrilling tale to tell back home about the *help* they had had from an unseen visitor, especially in that last harrowing thirty-six hours'

March. 'Lost, over the mountains'; and then he added, in his thoughts, 'but if there is only one man dead when we eventually arrive, the help and guiding presence, would count for nothing. '

Finally arriving back at Elephant Island, after many more trials and tribulations, they were overjoyed to find all the men were safe and had proved themselves to be of 'superior excellence'. Seamen, with such courage and initiative as they battled countless storms, and ill health and no doubt heart-ache as to 'how many more months' or 'will we ever be rescued' … they had been away almost two years.

Cheering loudly, the men watched in excitement as the rescue ship drew closer, then lowered a boat and in her was Shackleton. Tears were very near but when he found that every one of the men left behind had survived, he was elated!

In one hour the entire company of Elephant Island and their few belongings were aboard the rescue ship. The relief for Shackleton showed. Years seemed to drop from him as he stood before them. Now they could tell their amazing story to their country – to the world! And not one man lost.

★

Appendix – to complete the tale of 'shenanigans' at Southampton Airport that gave me:-

PROOF of CONNECTION,
with the 'other side'.

To go back to the beginning of this chapter and to the amazing experience I had through Reggie, a complete stranger. We were in the departure lounge of Southampton airport as he was about to depart on his home flight to Dublin.

I had been talking to his wife, also a complete stranger, when she asked me – noticing my notebooks and papers – was I a writer?

I only said a few words about it while Reggie was preoccupied with his laptop and papers anyway, As he stood up to leave he made a move towards me calling out as he did so 'Shelleck or Shelley, something like that anyway, and 'you must do it', 'write it down – sheelick' – over and over again.

Completely confused and amazed I signalled to him as clearly as I could, waving pen and paper, 'Yes I will. I WILL,' while having absolutely no idea of what this was all about.

He had, at first, put me in mind of Marty and Alice, also from Dublin, another couple of close London friends but this, with Jean, was to give amazing proof of survival and a continuation of friendship after so called death.

Many years earlier, Jean had tried hard to interest me in the story of Shackleton and his Antarctic expedition, even to buying me the poetry book and a recording of the relevant poem, 'The Waste Land', knowing my great interest in 'the other side', to the point of writing about it. As Jean knew, here was a great story of bravery and adventure and with a perfect story of the supernatural thrown in for good measure! I missed the point, ignored it and only now, years later, have I, through Reggie, a complete stranger, 'bullying' me to look into it, thoroughly enjoyed the book, the whole experience and the poem, which I would love to share with you now. 'The Waste Land' by T. S. Eliot.

Who is the third who walks always beside you?
When I count, there are only you and I together
But when I look ahead up the white road
There is always another one walking beside you
Gliding wrapt in a brown mantle, hooded
I do not know whether a man or a woman
—BUT who is that on the other side of you?

CHAPTER SEVEN

'For it is in giving that we receive
And it is in dying that we are born to Eternal Life.

St Francis

WHY DO YOU THINK there is still a great fascination among people (and this was all very popular centuries ago in Tudor England), to read their Star Signs; to visit a fortune teller and have their palms read or hear the wisdom of a Tarot Card reading, and of course, a real love of sayings? Sayings in whatever shape or form?

Recently I was in touch with a man who was upset because he was sure that he had 'let a few people down'. Try as we did, we could not convince him that he had not let anyone down, what happened was just 'one of those things' that happens and is out of our control. Still he was miserable about it, still convinced that he was at fault. It was not until we put the saying to him, 'You can't fail if you try. Not to try is to fail,' that we saw a glimmer of light in his eyes as we repeated, strongly, 'Not to try is to fail.' He did listen, thought about it and finally agreed.

Sayings, yes, are still as popular as ever. Therapists use them as comfort, help, advice for patients going through a tough time and many a one keeps a favourite list of them tucked safely away to bring out and read over again for comfort or advice – or both. They can be written out and kept in a little pocket book, or purse or even under a pillow, handy to pull out and read during some long, sleepless night.

Following on from here is a list of excellent sayings that were saved from the dustbin by Joe.

Joe is the proprietor of a computer store in the north of England (Geordie Land). He has a cupboard in the store that has been kept for years just for old rubbish customers have left behind and don't want anyway, and these are things that have not seen the light of day for years.

A lovely kind, caring man, Joe decided he had to have a clear out of this cupboard and finally, after many interruptions, got started. He was doing well, until, he picked up a disc along with the other rubbish, glanced at it and made to throw it away (along with all the other rubbish). He could not do it. He had to have another look at it (the writing), studied it again, and wanted to play it. Joe stressed to me the fact that he has never felt like that before over all the years, when he has thrown loads of such 'leftovers' away...so he played it. I know he will not mind me saying that he felt so moved by it all, the tears he only held back with great difficulty.

Here now, and at great expense (only joking), are these special sayings. Sorry we can't have the music or the beautiful scenery they were set in, but we have the words, and after all, that is what this is all about, words.

I wish you the strength of all elements.

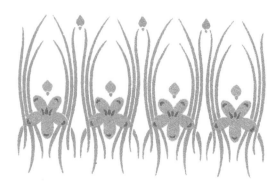

The one who takes your hand but touches your heart is a true Friend.

We seldom think of what we have, but always think of what we miss.

Don't cry because it's over now, laugh because it happened.

The more precisely you plan, the harder destiny will hit you.

What happens, happens for a reason.

Don't make an effort because the best things happen, when you least expect them.

The most difficult lesson to learn is: Which bridge in life to use or which one to break off.

The greatest events aren't the loudest, but the most quiet hours.

Everybody sees how you seem, however, only some know who you are.

He who would like to have something he never had, will have to do something well, that he hasn't done yet.

Perhaps God would want you to become acquainted with many different people in the course of your life, so that when you meet the right ones, you can appreciate and be grateful for them.

Plan for
tomorrow but
LIVE for today.

Love doesn't require two people look at each other, but that they look together in the same direction.

Life is drawing without an eraser.

I wish you always:
Air to breath,
Fire to warm you,
Water to drink and
The earth to live in.

For all my friends family and neighbours.
I hope you enjoyed it and have a great LIFE!

Sincerely, and with love and best wishes to you all.

From

Proprietor Joe, Publisher Jane, and me, Mary.

Thank you.